The Virgin Mary's
Got Nits

The Virgin Mary's Got Nits

A Christmas Anthology

Gervase Phinn

Illustrations by Matthew Phinn

HODDER

First published in Great Britain in 2014 by Hodder & Stoughton
An Hachette UK company

First published in paperback in 2016

1

A CIP catalogue record for this title is available from the British Library

ISBN 978 1 444 77940 0

Typeset in Adobe Caslon by Palimpsest Book Production Ltd,
Falkirk, Stirlingshire

Printed and bound by Clays Ltd, St Ives plc

Hodder & Stoughton policy is to use papers that are natural, renewable and
recyclable products and made from wood grown in sustainable forests. The logging
and manufacturing processes are expected to conform to the environmental
regulations of the country of origin.

Hodder & Stoughton Ltd
Carmelite House
50 Victoria Embankment
London EC4Y 0DZ

www.hodder.co.uk

For Sebastian Thaddeus Phinn

CONTENTS

THE STORY OF THE NATIVITY

THE NATIVITY PLAY IS OFF!

I approached an infant school nestled in the heart of the Yorkshire Dales one bitterly cold December afternoon. The surrounding fields and rocky outcrops were hidden under a smattering of snow and the belt of dark pines had a fine dusting of white. The air was icy fresh and the whole area around the small school was a vast white silent sea.

I had been invited by the head teacher, a large jolly woman with the wonderfully-Dickensian name of Miss Sally Precious, to see the rehearsal of the infant Nativity play.

As I walked up the path to the school, careful not to

slip on the icy surface, I was met by a group of small children chattering excitedly and apparently on their way home. I stopped a small boy with a shock of ginger hair, close set dark brown eyes and a missing front tooth. A small green candle of mucus appeared from his crusty nostril.

'Excuse me,' I said.

'We're not supposed to speak to strange men outside school,' he replied vociferously and regarding me suspiciously. He sniffed noisily and wiped his nose on the back of his hand.

'I'm here to see the Nativity play,' I told him.

'Well, it's off!' he told me bluntly.

'It's off?' I repeated.

The boy raised his hand to his head and scratched his scalp. 'Aye, t'Virgin Mary's got nits!'

THE INFANT NATIVITY PLAY

This innocence of young children is wonderfully illustrated at Christmas when the infant Nativity takes place in many schools throughout the country. Small children acting out one of the greatest stories of all time captures the very essence of Christmas. To see Mary, aged six, draped in a pale blue gown and cradling a large doll representing Baby Jesus never fails to bring a tear to the eye. To see Joseph, wide-eyed and innocent-faced, in a tartan dressing gown and a thick multi-coloured towel over his head held in place with an elastic belt with a snake clasp always brings a sympathetic smile to the lips. Then there are the shepherds, a motley group of children, also attired in dressing gowns and towels, the three kings wearing their cardboard crowns and clutching their gifts and the angels clad in white sheets and tinsel halos.

The delight of the infant Nativity is in the mix of childlike innocence and amusing mishaps. It is hard for the audience not to laugh when another Joseph wearing a brown poncho, which is clearly too big for a small child, treads on the bottom and falls over or when the angry little girl, masked by another infant dressed in brown and green, shouts off stage, 'Can you tell the palm tree to shift, Miss, he's blocking my view and I can't see my Nana.' At one Nativity play an over-enthusiastic little boy dressed in a soldier outfit and taking on the part of the Little Drummer Boy, proceeded to bang the metal drum around his neck loudly and with gusto. Anyone could see that the girl playing Mary was getting increasingly annoyed. Finally she placed Baby Jesus carefully back in the manger (a large pink doll with frizzy hair) and shouted at the boy, 'Will you shurrup Darren! I'm trying to gerrim off to sleep. You're doin' mi 'ead in!'

For one Nativity play the teachers (or more likely the parents) had really gone to town on the costumes for the children who played the Three Kings. The three little boys entered the stage in regal splendour, resplendent in designer outfits and holding their precious gifts. One child wore a huge silver turban and red cloak embellished with sequins and feathers and a second wore a circlet of gold. The third king sported a most impressive bejewelled crown. The jewels were in fact coloured wine gums which had been glued on to look like rubies and emeralds but they shone brilliantly under the lights.

As the play progressed, the third king began to get rather bored and started yawning and scratching and stretching. Then he proceeded to detach the fruit gums one by one from his crown, pop them in his mouth and chew them vigorously. The other two kings watched him with interest. Finally the second king leaned over and said in a loud stage whisper, 'Give us one Jason.' The third king obliged. The drama concluded with the children singing, 'Oh little town of Bethlehem' accompanied by the loud chomping of the Magi.

At the conclusion of one infant Nativity play, Mary and Joseph sat at the centre of a colourful tableau of kings, shepherds and animals (the last being children in cardboard sheep and donkey masks). A group of little angels in white crêpe paper and cardboard headbands with silver stars on the front stood on a raised platform at the back. As the teacher at the piano struck up with the introduction to 'Away in a Manger' Mary rocked Baby Jesus – another large pink doll with frizzy hair and eyes which opened and closed – and the doll (one of the talking variety) started to cry and asked for its nappy to be

changed. Mary shook it forcefully to shut it up which only resulted in the doll repeatedly crying and demanding to be changed. Mary in desperation pushed the doll roughly into Joseph's hands. 'You have him,' she said. 'He won't shut up!' The small boy playing Joseph looked at a loss what to do as the doll continued to cry and demand to be changed. He shook the doll so forcefully that the head became detached from the body and bounced down the stage just as the angels got to the line in the carol, 'The Little Lord Jesus lay down his sweet head.' One of the three kings quickly retrieved the head and passed it to Mary who reunited it with its body. To the sound of laughter from the audience and the crying of the doll, the angels continued to sing lustily. 'The stars in the bright sky looked down as he lay, the little Lord Jesus asleep on the hay.'

THE VISIT OF THE SCHOOL INSPECT OR

This morning, children, we have a special visitor in school.
He's sitting at the back of the hall.
His name in Mr Leatherboy and he's a school inspector
Come to watch the rehearsal for our Nativity Play.
I am sure he will leave us very much impressed.
I don't think he will be very much impressed
By what you are doing Malcolm Biggerdyke.
Donkeys don't roll about on the floor making silly
    noises,
Now do they? They stand up straight and pay attention.
Justine don't do that with Baby Jesus, dear,
And Philip, please stop fiddling with the frankincense.
How do you mean you've got your finger stuck in the
    hole in the lid?
Well how did you manage to do that?
My goodness, that was a silly thing to do, wasn't it?
Well, if it went in it must come out, wiggle it about a bit.
No, I don't mean your bottom, wiggle your finger about.
He doesn't need your help thank you very much Harry.

Yes, I know you are only trying to be helpful.

Just leave the lid alone and put your crown on straight.

Justine, I have asked you not to do that with Baby Jesus,

And Gavin, will you stop that immediately!

Crooks are for holding sensibly and not for swinging
about.

You will have someone's eye out.

Angela dear, I really don't think the Angel of the Lord

Would wipe her nose on her sleeve, now would she?

Use a tissue. Well go and get one from Mrs Tricklebank.

Tyrone, palm trees stand still, they do not wander
about the stage.

Go back and stand on your spot and don't wave your
fronds about.

Justine, I shall not tell you again not to do that with
Baby Jesus.

Jonathan Jones, why are you pulling that silly face?

One day the wind will change and it will stay like
that.

Yes, I know you didn't want to be Joseph,

Yes, I know you wanted to be the grumpy Innkeeper,

But there are some things in life many of us don't want
to do

And we just have to grin and bear it and not pull silly
    faces.

Duane, I did ask you not to wear those red trainers.

Herod wouldn't be wearing shoes which light up and
    flash

Now would he? No, you can't wear your wellingtons.

What is it Justine? Well, I did tell you not to do that
    with Baby Jesus.

Put him back in the crib and leave him alone.

I am sure we will fix his head back on before the
    performance.

Well, I think we are about ready to start, Mr Leatherboy.

Oh dear, he appears to have gone.

THE YORKSHIRE NATIVITY

I sat in pride of place at the back of the large room as the children performed their drama on the makeshift stage. Of all the nativity plays I have seen over the years this was undoubtedly one of the most original and perhaps the most memorable. The cast had dispensed with the usual attire: sandals, dressing gowns, pasteboard crowns, coloured towels draped over heads, cotton wool beards, cloaks, cardboard wings and tinsel halos and had opted for simple modern dress.

A large, fresh-faced girl with long flaxen hair, attired in black slacks and a white blouse stood at the side of the stage as two children, the boy dressed in jeans and denim jacket, the girl in a bright flowery dress, entered holding hands.

'And it came to pass,' said the narrator, 'that a decree went out from Caesar Augustus, the Emperor in Rome, that all the world should be taxed and Joseph, the carpenter, took Mary, his wife, who was having a baby, from Galilee to the city of David which is called Bethlehem, in Judea from where his family came. They walked wearily along the hot and dusty road and into the town, which was crowded with people all there to be counted. Very soon Mary and Joseph, tired from their long journey, arrived at an inn looking for somewhere to stay.'

A boy wearing a blue and white striped apron stepped on stage, his hands on his hips.

'Innkeeper! Innkeeper! 'As thy any room?' asked Joseph.

'Nay, lad,' replied the Innkeeper. 'I've nowt left. We're full to burstin'. Place is chock-a block wi' folk cum to pay their taxes.'

'That's a rum do. We've been on t'rooad all day,' Joseph told him, 'and both of us are fair fit to drop. We're fair fagged out!'

'Well. I'm reight sorry, lad, but there's nowt I can give thee. We're full up for t'neet.'

'I've got t'wife out 'ere,' announced Joseph. 'An' she's 'avin' a babby, tha knaas.'

'I'm reight sorry abaat that, an' all,' said the Innkeeper, 'but there's no room in t'inn, and that's top an' bottom of it.'

'Nowt at all?'

'Theer's t'stable round t'back. Bit basic like, but it's

warm and dry enough. Tha can sleep theer if tha wants.'

'It'll 'ave to do,' said Joseph. 'Come on Mary.'

The narrator took up the story. 'And so Mary and Joseph had to sleep in the barn with the oxen and the asses, for there was no room in the inn that night.'

The holy couple left the stage and two boys and a girl entered. 'Now nearby, in a distant dale, on a dark, cold night, three shepherds were tending their sheep and watching over their flocks, when suddenly there appeared, in the dark sky, a great shining light.'

'Hey up!' said the first shepherd, 'tek a look at that then!'

'Weer?' asked the second shepherd.

'Theer.'

'Weer?'

'Theer up yonder in t'sky.'

'Wor is it?'

'I don't know but it's gerrin' brighter.'

A girl entered in a white blouse and skirt. 'Hey up, lads! Don't be frit. I'm not gunna hurt thee. I'm Hangel o' Lord, 'ere wi' tidin's of gret joy.'

'What's that then?' asked the third shepherd.

'There's a babby boy been booarn toneet, a reight

special babby, who's liggin in a manger, wrapped up in swaddling bands, over in Bethle'em. God's own lad, Saviour o' World, Christ the Lord, the Messiah, and does thy know what?'

'What?' asked the first shepherd.

''E's a reight bobby-dazzler, that's what.'

'Way, 'appen we berrer gu an' see 'im then, sithee,' said the first shepherd.

'Wor abaat t'tups and yows?' asked the second. 'I'm not reight chuffed abaat leavin' 'em on their own what wi' wolves.'

'Ne'er thee mither abaat tha sheep,' said the angel, 'I'll see to 'em fer thee.'

The narrator stepped forward and a group of children came on stage. 'And suddenly the sky was filled with a host of heavenly angels.' The children sang lustily, 'Glory to God, Glory to God, Glory to God in the highest and on Earth peace and goodwill toward all men.' As the angels and shepherds left the stage, the three kings entered. 'Now far far away in a distant land three kings, wise men of the East, saw a star high in the dark sky which foretold of the birth of the new-born king.'

'Hey up!' said the first king, 'tek a look at that then!'

'Weer?' asked the second king.

'Theer.'

'Weer?'

'Theer up yonder in t'sky.'

'Wor is it?'

'By the heck, it's a reight big star.'

'Tha knaas what that means, dun't tha?' said the third king.

'No,' chorused the other two.

'Tha does!'

'We doaan't.'

'Summat special's 'appenin' that's what. It's a sign from on 'igh. A new babby king's been born toneet. It were foretold. Come on lads, let's follow yonder star and see weer it teks us.'

'Hold up,' said the second king. 'We shall 'ave to tek 'im a present.' The three kings left the stage and picked up three brightly wrapped parcels.

'So the three kings set off following the star,' said the narrator, 'carrying their gifts of gold, frankincense and myrrh and soon they arrived at a huge marble palace.' The three kings appeared back on stage. 'They knocked loudly on the great iron door and from inside came a voice. It was King Herod.'

'Clear off!'

'Oppen dooer!' shouted the first king. 'We're t'three kings from t'Orient.'

'I don't care who thy are or weer tha from. Clear off!'

'We've got gret news that a new babby king 'as been born this neet an' we're off to see 'im? Does tha want to come wi' us?'

On stage came a small boy with spiky hair and a brightly coloured shirt. 'What's all this abaat a babby king then?' he asked.

'I've just telled thee,' said the first king. 'See that theer star up in t'sky?'

'Weer?' asked Herod.

'Theer.'

'Weer?'

'Theer up yonder in t'sky.'

'Wor abaat it?'

'Well it's tekkin us to see this new babby king. Get tha cooat on and tha can come wi' us.'

'Nay, I'll not bother,' replied Herod, 'but cum back this way will tha an' tell me weer this babby is and 'appen

I'll go an' see 'im mi sen and tek 'im a present.' He turned to the audience and pulled a gruesome face. 'I'll tck' im a present, all reight, and it'll not be wor 'e's hexpectin', I'll tell thee that. I'm not reight chuffed abaat this at all. There's only gunna be one king around 'ere sithee and that's gunna be mc.' Herod stomped off.

The narrator continued as the stage filled with the children who gathered around a small manger. 'And that night, in a stable in Bethlehem, Jesus Christ was born and the Three Wise Men and the humble shepherds, the angels and the beasts of the fields worshipped him for he was the Son of God, the most wonderful, the King of all Kings and the Light of the World.'

'Glory bc to God,' chorused the children.

'And all who saw the child marvelled,' said the narrator finally, 'but Mary, holding her new born baby close to her breast, kept all these things to herself and pondered them in her heart.'

NO ROOM AT THE INN

Mary in a pale blue cloak,
Joseph with a towel over his head,
Approached the cardboard Inn
And knocked.

'Have you a room?' asked Joseph.
'Sorry,' said the Innkeeper, shaking his little head.
'But we have travelled far,' said Joseph.
'No room at the Inn.'
'And we are tired, very tired.'
'We are all full up and have no room.'
'And my dear wife is to have a baby.'
'We have no room at the Inn,' said the Innkeeper.
'Oh please,' begged Joseph, 'just for the night.'

The Innkeeper,
In a pale brown dressing gown
And bright red slippers,
Observed the little travellers

Sad and weary and far from home
And scratched his head.
'Have my room,' he said smiling,
'And I'll sleep in the stable.'

PICTURES OF CHRISTMAS

The infant children had been asked to illustrate the Christmas story. One small child had produced a large very colourful effort of Mary and Joseph making their way to Bethlehem. Joseph walked ahead of his wife who was perched on a small donkey. Behind Mary in the picture sat a huge hairy creature with large yellow eyes and long black feelers.

'What's that in the picture?' I asked the child, indicating the monstrous creature behind Mary.

'The flea,' replied the child nonchalantly.

'The flea?' I repeated.

'You know the flea, what went with Mary and Joseph,' explained the child. 'Miss said that the Angel of the Lord told Mary and Joseph when they left Bethlehem to take the baby and flea to Egypt.'

Another illustration by a young child featured the traditional Christmas scene with Mary, Joseph, and Baby Jesus, surrounded by adoring kings and shepherds. Peering into the crib in pride of place was a large red-faced individual with a fat, smiling face.

'Who is this?' asked the intrigued teacher.

'Round John Virgin,' replied the child.

In another picture, this time of the stable, a child had carefully drawn all the various people and animals gathered around the crib. Behind one of the kings was a large tortoise, its great wrinkled head poking out of its shell.

The bemused teacher commented that it was the first time she had seen a tortoise at the Nativity scene.

'Well,' replied the child, 'when we say the Lord's Prayer in assembly it says, "This is the prayer of Jesus' tortoise".'

THE LITTLE ANGEL

He looked like a little angel,
With his round eyes as blue as the sky
And an innocent childlike expression.
He peered through the curtains at the assembled
    parents,
Dressed in his white silk costume trimmed with
    silver
And waited for his entrance.
He turned to his friend and whispered:
'If Miss thinks I'm being a flipping snowflake
    next year
She's got another think coming!'

DRAMA IN THE STABLE

One Nativity play was, without doubt, the most dramatic retelling of the Christmas story I have ever seen.

Everything went smoothly until the arrival of the Three Kings. The second king, close on the heels of the little boy in front of him, trod on the first king's cloak (a faded red velvet curtain still with the curtain hooks in). The first king swivelled around, pushed the second in the chest and told him to 'gerroff mi flippin' cloak' although the adjective 'flipping' was not the word he actually used. The second king hit the first over the head with the frankincense (a large plastic shampoo bottle full of coloured sand). The first king retaliated by hitting the second with the gift of gold (a Tupperware box covered in golden wrapping paper). Then the third king joined in the fray and all three were soon rolling about on the floor. A hunched figure (the teacher) appeared and, gathering up the three little boys, manhandled them off the stage. The play continued with Mary whispering to Joseph loud enough for the audience to hear, 'Where are t'Three Kings?'

'They've got done,' replied the boy playing Joseph, 'and been sent home.'

MARY

In another school I discovered a small girl of about five or six who had just taken the part of an angel in the Nativity play. She was a pale-faced child dressed in a flowing white silk robe, large paper wings and a crooked tinsel halo, sitting in the entrance hall of the school. The little girl was clearly distressed for her cheeks were wet with tears and she was wiping her nose on her sleeve and sobbing.

'Now whatever is the matter?' I asked gently. 'It can't be that bad.'

'It is!' cried the girl.

'What is your name?' I asked.

'It's Mary,' replied the child.

'Well I've just seen you on stage,' I told her, 'and I thought you were a little star.'

'I wasn't a little star,' she replied sharply. 'I was an angel.'

'I meant you were very good.'

'No, I wasn't,' she sniffed.

'And why are you crying, Mary?' I asked.

'Because they keep calling me virgin and I don't like it.'

'There is nothing so affecting,' wrote the poet Coleridge, 'as the innocence of small children.'

THE THREE KINGS

The infant Nativity play is often a good-humoured, sometimes very moving and on occasions an extremely funny moment in the school calendar. It is a joyous event when the little ones, attired in a motley assortment of coloured towels and scarves, dressing gowns and paper crowns, cardboard wings and tinsel halos, wriggle and scratch and smile and wave and move the audience to laughter and sometimes tears.

One school performance, however, was a very serious affair. It was clear that the head teacher had drilled the children with military precision not to fidget, twiddle with their hair, move around the stage, poke their noses, talk amongst themselves and, above all, not to giggle or smile. In this production Mary's face looked set in stone, Joseph's countenance was like a death mask, the shepherds gazed glumly and the archangel Gabriel stood unsmiling and with her hands clasped in front of her.

The first of the three kings entered the stage.

'I am Melchior, King of the North,' he said solemnly.

'I have travelled from afar,
Following yonder shining star,
To celebrate upon this day
The Christ child sleeping in the hay,
And for this child this gift I bring
Worthy of the new-born king.'
He paused dramatically. 'My gift is gold,' he said,
Enter the second kind equally po-faced.
'I am Balthazar King of the West,' he announced.
'On this cold and frosty night,
I've followed the star which shines so bright,
To this stable cold and bare,
To find the child who lieth there,
The baby sleeping in the hay,
And for this child this gift I bring,
Worthy of the new-born king.'
He too paused dramatically. 'My gift is frankincense,'
he said.

The third king strode into the stage with a broad grin
on his face. I could see the head teacher shuffle uncomfortably in his chair for this child (and there is always one)
had patently failed to listen to the teacher's instruction to
remain serious-faced. The boy was a massively freckled

child who wore large coloured glasses and he had long ginger hair which escaped from beneath his crown.

'I am Gaspar, King of the South,' he said jauntily before puffing out his cheeks as if exhausted.

'Beyond the mountain ranges high
I saw a star up in the sky
And followed it from a distant land,
Over seas of shifting sand,
To pay my homage to this child,
Who lay in the manger meek and mild.
And for this child this gift I bring
Worthy of the new-born king.'

Like the other two kings he paused for effect but continued to beam at the audience.

'My gift,' he said loudly, 'is mirth.'

As I sat there in the school hall I peered for a moment through the window at the jet black sky sprinkled with stars and reflected on that first Nativity. What better gift to bring to the world, I thought, than the gift of mirth.

2

MEMORIES OF CHRISTMAS

A SPECIAL TIME OF YEAR

Chill in the air,
Hoar frost,
Roaring wind,
Ice on the road,
Snow on the roof,
Travellers from afar.
Mother and child,
Angels in the sky,
Starlight.

A CHILD'S CHRISTMAS

Christmas for me when I was a boy was, as I guess it is for most children, a very special time and my father and mother made a great effort in our house to have everything just right for the occasion. They would increase my pocket money for me to buy presents and before the big day take me shopping into Rotherham. I loved those visits into town just before Christmas when the shop windows were stacked with Christmas goods, when coloured lights lit up the streets and carol singers and the Salvation Army band filled All Saints' Square with music. It was even more special with a light dusting of snow covered pavements and rootops making the dark town seem so much cleaner and brighter. I loved it when the air became so icy it burnt your cheeks and your exhaled breath came in great clouds.

The old imitation Christmas tree would be taken from its dusty box and erected in the front room to be decorated with coloured balls, little wooden figures and tinsel and we children were allowed to drape streamers in the living room and put up balloons. The crib with the small plaster Nativity figures was given pride of place on the mantelpiece and the crucifix on the wall was taken down until the New Year.

One year my father was persuaded by Mr Evans to have a real Christmas tree.

Our neighbour said he had a contact in the Forestry Commission at Clumber Park and could provide one at a fair price. He didn't mention just how big the tree would be. We were expecting a small affair so when this strangely-shaped monstrosity arrived my mother was less than pleased and stared in disbelief as it was manoeuvred through the back gate. It was all of eight foot high with great spreading lateral branches and twisting roots.

'We won't get it in the house, never mind the front room,' my mother complained.

'Not to worry,' said Dad. 'I'll chop a bit off when I get back from work.'

Alec, my brother, prevailed upon Dad to let us cut a bit off and when he had departed for the afternoon shift, we set to work with the saw. The bit we lopped off the tree was from the top so we had this strange looking truncated Christmas tree emerging from a silver bucket which shed its needles as soon as was placed in the corner of the front room. This was the very last real Christmas tree we bought.

Like most children, when I was young I loved Christmas more than any other occasion in the year. It was so much more to me than just the presents and the delicious food. Shop windows in Rotherham would be ablaze with colour and illuminations would stretch along the high street to brighten up the otherwise dark and solid industrial Yorkshire town. All Saints' Square, with the great medieval sandstone church towering above, would resound with piped carol music and people would seem friendlier somehow. The whole house would smell of cooked ham, mince pies and fruitcake and outside in the cold street there seemed to be something special in the air. The excitement and anticipation of Christmas never ever waned for me when I was young.

CHRISTMAS MASS

On Christmas morning the whole family would walk through the town to St Bede's Church, a good couple of miles or so from home. On the exterior it was dark and ugly but inside it was another world. It was here that as a young boy I had my first introduction to indoor beauty, of ornament, ostentation, spectacle and mystery. It was like entering a magical world of burnished metal, gilt, stone and polished wood. There were great brightly coloured plaster statues staring serenely down from their plinths, a flickering red light hanging in a casket of gold above the tabernacle, heavy wooden pews redolent with lavender polish and camphor, rows of shining candles and on the great high altar draped in white linen was an ornate golden cross. Then there was the smell of incense and the chanting of the Latin which for a child was mysterious and magical.

High Mass on Christmas morning was a very special occasion at St Bede's. Beneath the altar decorated with white winter roses and holly with blood red berries was the crib with life-size figures of Mary and Joseph, the shepherds and kings, angels and the ox and the ass all gathered around the manger containing a pink-faced baby Jesus.

At one memorable Christmas Mass the priest, draped in a gold cope and accompanied by altar boys in red and white, processed around the church. The organ roared and those in the choir raised their voices as the priest sprinkled copious amounts of holy water to the right and left, dipping the aspergillum (a brass stick with a round knob on the end) in the brass receptacle and dousing the congregation. He did this with a vengeance, spattering faces and clothes with liberal amounts of holy water. One parishioner at the end of a pew was not filled with Christmas spirit when her new pale blue suede coat got a thorough drenching. She uttered 'My God!' loud enough for all in her vicinity to hear. On this occasion, as the priest continued with his sprinkling, the round ball on the end of the brass stick shot off. Rumour has it that one of the altar boys, noticing that the knob screwed in to the top of the stick, had unscrewed it so that it was held on tenuously by a single thread. The brass ball flew through the air and with a resounding crack hit an elderly woman clutching her rosary beads smack on the back of her head.

'Jesus, Mary and Joseph!' cried the old woman, falling to her knees. 'I've been struck!'

Such was the priest's authority and his hold on the congregation that no one dared laugh. Fortunately she was not badly hurt and he continued to process around the church, apparently unconcerned by the interruption, as the choir sang: 'Come, come, come to the manger.'

THE PALM TREE

I was visiting my home town of Rotherham one Saturday before Christmas and met Miss Greenwood, my former infant teacher, in All Saints' Square. She was now over eighty years old but still possessed the shining eyes and the gentle smile of the great teacher she was. I loved Miss Greenwood and those early years at school. I moulded little clay models, dug in the sand pit, played in the water tray, counted with little coloured beads, sang the nursery rhymes, danced with bare feet in the hall, made models with toilet rolls and cardboard boxes, splashed poster paint on large sheets of grey sugar paper, chanted poems and listened to stories and learnt to read. And how I loved those stories she read to us in the Reading Corner. I would be the first to snuggle up on a large bean bag to listen enrapt to *The Tale of Peter Rabbit*, *The Flowers of St Francis*, *Noddy*, *Little Black Sambo*, *The Parables of Jesus*, *Alice in Wonderland*, *The Water Babies* and *Tales from the Brothers Grimm*. At Christmas she would read the narrative poem, *The Night Before Christmas*, the story of

The Little Match Girl which brought tears to her eyes, and that part of *A Christmas Carol* (simplified version of course) where Scrooge, seeing the error of his ways, celebrated Christmas for the first time in many years.

That Saturday I had taken Miss Greenwood for afternoon tea in Davy's Cafe in All Saints' Square and we had reminisced.

'It's so lovely to see you again, Miss Greenwood,' I had told her.

'Is it really?' she had asked. She had sounded genuinely surprised.

'Well of course, Miss Greenwood. I have so many happy memories of my early schooldays.'

'I think under the circumstances, Gervase,' she had said, 'you *can* call me Dorothy.'

'No, no, I couldn't,' I had replied. 'I could never call you Dorothy.'

'Why ever not?'

'Because you were my teacher, Miss Greenwood.' Then I had added, 'And I loved you. I loved coming to school, I loved all your lessons and any success I have had, I owe to my parents and to dedicated teachers like you.'

She had smiled. 'And do you remember when you wet yourself, Gervase?' she had asked with a twinkle in her eyes.

'Of course I do. How could I ever forget?'

I was not a particularly clever or confident child, never the bright little button who sat on the top table with his hand always in the air to answer the teacher's questions, the talented artist, sharp at number work, the good speller, the one who wins all the cups, captains the school team, takes the lead part in the school play. I was a member of the unremarkable majority – the average pupil, the big hump in the academic bell, the 'nothing special' sort of child, ordinary, biddable, quiet. And when it came to the Christmas nativity play, I was never Joseph, the Innkeeper, one of the Three Wise Men or the First Shepherd. I was usually one of the extras.

The time I wet myself will remain ingrained in my memory. The curtains had opened on the Christmas nativity play and there I had stood, six years old, stiff as a lamp post. I was the palm tree, encased in brown crêpe paper with two big bunches of papier mâché coconuts dangling from my neck and a clump of bright green cardboard leaves in each hand and arranged like a crown on my head. I had stared at all the faces in the audience and had wriggled nervously. Then someone had laughed and it had started off others laughing too. It was the first occasion anyone had laughed at me and I had felt so alone and upset. I had looked for my parents and, seeing them in the second row, I had focused on them. They, of course, were not laughing. I had begun to cry and then, frozen under the bright lights and frightened, I had wet myself. It had seeped through the brown crêpe paper leaving a large dark stain in the front. The audience only laughed louder. I had been devastated. On the way home, my face wet with tears, my father had held my small hand between his great fat fingers and told me that I had been the best palm tree he had ever seen. My mother had told me that I was the star of the show. I knew at the time full well that they had not been telling me the truth, but it had been so good to be told. I felt so secure and so loved.

'And do you remember, Miss Greenwood,' I had asked her, 'what you said to me when I came off the stage?'

'I don't,' she had said. 'Remind me.'

'Well, I guess some teachers would have stabbed the

air angrily with a finger and told that little boy what a silly child he was and demanded to know why he hadn't gone to the toilet before going on stage.'

'And what did I say?' she had asked.

'You put your arm around me and then said, "Don't worry, love, I used to wet my knickers when I was your age."'

There was a short silence. Then a small smile came to my former teacher's lips. 'Well, Gervase,' she had said, 'it comes full circle.'

3

THE VISIT FROM SANTA CLAUS

FATHER CHRISTMAS

'Children should be told the truth,' the Chairman of the school's Governing Body told me. 'Telling lies to the young is wrong. To have children believe in some mythical red coated figure with a woolly beard or a fairy that takes your tooth from under the pillow is deceitful. Children should be spared such nonsense.'

I begged to differ. Father Christmas and the Tooth Fairy are part of childhood. It would be a sad world indeed if the only thing children encounter as they grow up is the bald dull truth. For young children everything in the world is new and different, exciting and colourful and they will have to grapple with the grim realities of life soon enough, so in childhood let them have a bit of magic and myth.

SANTA'S REINDEERS

Mrs Ross, the deputy head teacher at the infant school, telephoned to ask if I would play Father Christmas. She had been let down by the Caretaker, who always took on the role but he was in hospital having broken a leg falling from the ladder when putting up the Christmas lights on the tree. She sounded desperate, so reluctantly I agreed. In the staffroom I donned the ill-fitting costume and cotton-wool beard and was all set to enter the hall where the small children were assembled when Mrs Ross stopped me.

'Where are your boots?' she asked.

'Boots?', I repeated.

'Father Christmas has to have boots.'

'I didn't bring any,' I replied feebly.

'Oh well,' she said, 'you'll have to take those brown shoes off and go barefoot.'

'Could I keep my socks on?' I asked.

'No, it will have to be bare feet and you will have to make something up and explain why you have no boots.'

When I entered the hall the little children squealed

with delight when they saw the familiar red coat and white cotton-wool beard. Everything was going well until a bright little spark announced loudly, 'You're not real, you know.'

'Oh yes, I am!' I replied in a deep jolly Father Christmas voice.

'Oh no, you're not,' she persisted, 'your beard's held on by elastic. I can see it. And Father Christmas has big boots. You're not wearing boots. You've got bare feet.'

'Ah, well, I got stuck in a snowdrift on my way here and my boots were so filled up with snow that I had to take them off to dry them.'

'Well, where are they then?' asked a child.

'The school caretaker is drying them out in front of his fire.'

'He hasn't got a fire,' piped up another child. 'It's smokeless on the estate.'

'Well on his pipes then.'

'You're not the real Father Christmas!' continued the first child, obstinately shaking her little head.

'Oh yes, I am!' I said in my loud, jolly voice and heard a whole school hall shout back: 'Oh no, you're not!'

Mrs Ross intervened and bailed me out by starting the

singing. After three verses of 'Rudolf the Red-nosed Reindeer' each child came forward to receive a small present.

'What are the names of your reindeers?' asked a little boy.

'Well, there's Rudolf,' I started, 'and Donner and Blitzen and er ... er ...'

The deputy head teacher, seeing that I was struggling, helped me out again by explaining that Father Christmas was rather deaf.

'Some of the snow from the snowdrift is still in his ears,' she said.

One child asked me if I knew her name and when I replied that I did not she looked crestfallen. 'But I thought Father Christmas knows all the boys' and girls' names?'

Mrs Ross explained that Father Christmas's eyes weren't too good either and he had such a lot of letters to read.

One rather grubby little scrap asked if she could sit on my knee.

'No, Chelsea,' said the deputy head teacher firmly. 'I don't think—'. She was too late; the child had clambered up and clung to me like a little monkey.

'Come on down, Chelsea,' said Mrs Ross. 'I don't think Father Christmas wants children on his knee. He's got a poorly leg.' Any more ailments, I thought, and I would be joining the caretaker in the Moorgate Hospital.

'Now, you be a very good little girl and sit on the floor, Chelsea,' I said in my jolly voice, 'otherwise all the other children will want to climb up.' Chelsea stayed put and held fast like a limpet. I chuckled uneasily until the child's teacher managed to prise her off. Mrs Ross shrugged and looked knowingly at the teachers standing around the hall.

After the children had sung me out to 'Jingle Bells' I was invited into the staffroom. It was extremely hot under the red suit.

'Father Christmas, you were a great hit,' said the deputy head teacher. The staff looked on and nodded. 'And we'd like to give you a little Christmas gift.'

'Oh no,' I said, 'it really isn't necessary.'

'Oh, but it is necessary,' insisted Mrs Ross and presented me with a small bottle wrapped in bright Christmas paper.

I shook my gift and held it to my ear.

'Aftershave?' I enquired. 'Is it aftershave?'

'No, Father Christmas,' the staff replied.

'Is it a little bottle of whisky?'

'No, Father Christmas,' they chorused.

I tore off the wrapping to reveal a small brown bottle of medication. The label read: 'For infestation of the head.'

'Chelsea's just got over head lice,' said the head teacher. 'It's not advisable to be too close to her for the time being.'

'And she's just recovered from scabies,' piped up a beaming teacher. The rest of the staff then joined in with a hearty 'Ho! Ho! Ho!'

The following year I was asked to make a repeat visit as Father Christmas. This time I was well-prepared wearing a costume that fitted, a pair of large black rubber wellington boots and an impressive-looking white fluffy beard. I had also learnt all the names of the reindeers just in case another inquisitive child asked me again what their names were. I was also determined not to let any child clamber onto my knee.

Things went well until a little boy with a shock of red hair and a face full of freckles waved his hand in the air like a daffodil in a strong wind. He glowered at me as he sat crossed-legged in the front row.

'Yes, little boy,' I said in my deep jolly booming Father Christmas voice. 'What would you like to tell Santa Claus?'

'So, what happened to the bike I asked for last Christmas?' he demanded.

Stuttering some excuse I moved on and told the children how busy I was at Christmas with so many presents to deliver. When I was asked the names of my reindeers I rattled them off confidently and, seeing how impressed the teachers were, I have to admit I felt rather smug. One child raised her hand.

'And what about Olive?' she asked.

'Olive?' I repeated.

'The reindeer called Olive,' said the child. 'You've forgotten about her.'

I looked towards the teacher and shrugged. 'I don't think Father Christmas has a reindeer called Olive,' said the teacher.

'He does Miss,' replied the child. 'It says in the song: "Olive the other reindeer".'

SANTA SAN

My son Matthew spent several years in Hiroshima as an artist-in-residence. He stands out in Japan being tall and thin and wearing large round black-framed glasses. On his first morning at the high school where he was to teach, the principal asked him to address (in Japanese) the entire school – a rather daunting experience for a young man new to the country and new to teaching. Matthew climbed the steps to the stage with all eyes upon him but before he could open his mouth there was an audible gasp from the students who clapped their hands and exclaimed 'Aaaaahhh Hally Potter!'

Matthew volunteered to visit a local nursery school every few weeks to teach the young children aged between two and five years old. Usually he would do some activities such as painting, playing music on his guitar, telling the children stories and talking to them about life in England. One Christmas he agreed to dress as Santa Claus and donned a cheap outfit, black leather workman's gloves, heavy black boots and a fake cotton-wool beard. He walked down the school corridor with a sack over his back containing small presents for the children and saw all the excited little faces peering through the glass in the classroom windows.

One little boy of about four or five emerged from the toilet pulling up his pants, to be confronted by the tall red clad figure with the great white beard. He froze like a rabbit caught in a headlight's glare and looked absolutely terrified. He let go of his pants which fell to the floor. Then, when Matthew bent and said a hearty 'Ho, ho ho!' (which means absolutely nothing in Japanese), the child screamed and shuffled off at high speed down the corridor, his pants still around his ankles.

When Matthew was introduced to the older children they were fascinated by the unusual-looking visitor. He was asked many questions in Japanese: 'Where did he live?' 'Had he any children?' 'Where was his sleigh?' 'How many reindeers had he got?' Then one little girl broke the spell by demanding, 'Why is Santa San wearing Masshu Sensei's (Teacher Matthew's) glasses?'

THE COLOUR OF CHRISTMAS

Red for Santa's scarlet hood,
Red for the holly berries in the wood,
Red for the Robin's crimson breast,
Red is the colour I love the best.

Red for the wrapping paper bright,
Red for flames in the firelight,
Red for the stocking at the foot of the bed
It's the colour of Christmas, the colour red.

CHRISTMAS PRESENT

I do like bright colours. Red in particular is such a cheerful, uplifting hue. When my wife, Christine, was fifty I bought her some rather attractive lacy red silk underwear for Christmas. When she opened her present in front of our four grown-up children and my mother, the onlookers turned the very same colour of the said undergarments.

'Put them away, Christine!' snapped my mother. 'His father went through that stage!'

A BOOK AT CHRISTMAS

When I was little I would wake up on Christmas morning
to see the bulging pillow case at the bottom of the bed.
There would be a couple of tangerines, a string bag of
assorted nuts, chocolate coins encased in gold and silver
tin foil, a box of rose-scented Turkish delights covered in
powdery icing sugar and glistening dates in a strangely
shaped wooden box with three camels against an orange
sky on the front. There would be crystallised fruits, a
selection box of chocolates, coloured pencils, a John Bull
printing set, a rectangular tin of water colour paints and
two camel hair brushes, roller skates, a penknife, lead
soldiers and always a book. My books formed a precious
collection, my own little library, and I have them still. As
I look up from my desk now I see a shelf full of those
adventure stories my father bought for me when I was a
child: Anthony Hope's swashbuckling *The Prisoner of
Zenda* and *Rupert of Hentzau*, John Buchan's gripping
The Thirty Nine Steps, Chesterton's thrilling *The Man
Who Was Thursday*, Edgar Rice Burroughs' *Tarzan of the*

Apes, Erskine Childers' masterpiece, *The Riddle of the Sands*, and of course, *David Copperfield*.

One Christmas I found a copy of *Treasure Island* in my stocking. I loved to read myself, sometimes under the sheet with a torch (when I should have been sound asleep) but sometimes my father would read to me and that Christmas he read from the novel. I snuggled down, closed my eyes and listened spellbound as he lifted the text from the page. I remember the fear I felt inside when, at the age of eleven, I heard my father read that part of the novel when Jim first comes across Long John Silver. I felt something of Jim Hawkins' terror of 'the seafaring man with the one leg.'

How that personage haunted my dreams, I need scarcely tell you. On stormy nights, when the wind shook the four corners of the house and the surf roared along the cove and up the cliffs, I would see him in a thousand forms, and with a thousand diabolical expressions. Now the leg would be cut off at the knee, now the hip, now he was a monstrous kind of creature who had never had but the one leg and that in the middle of his body. To see him leap and run and pursue me over the hedge and ditch was the worst of nightmares.

As I listened to my father on that cold and blustery night I was there with Jim hiding from Long John Silver in the barrel of apples and overhearing his murderous plans. And when my father got to the most exciting part, just as the pirate was to discover the eavesdropper, my father snapped the book shut, ruffled my hair and said, 'Well goodnight.'

THE TREASURE

Opening the covers of a book
Is like lifting the lid of a treasure chest.
Look inside and you will find
Golden stories and glittering characters.

Some are given a map to show where X marks the spot.
Some are given the precious key to open the lock.
Some are helped to lift the heavy lid,
But for some it will remain a hidden treasure.

THE BOOK SIGNING

More books are given as presents at Christmas than at any other time of the year. People looking for that final present often opt for a book and if it is signed by the author then all the better. Publishers are keen to get their authors out and about at this time of year, signing in bookshops and speaking at literary events. Most authors have tales to tell about their signing sessions. Michael Parkinson for example was appearing at a book signing of his latest book when he overheard the following comment by a customer: 'I tell you what, he doesn't suit daylight, does he?'

My good friend the lawyer Stephen D. Smith recounts in his books (*Boozers, Ballcocks and Bail* and *Fiddlers, Fakers and Fleas*) many anecdotes about the amusing side of the legal profession. He tells the story of one occasion when he was in a shop to sign his latest book. He was placed at a small table in front of a large publicity poster announcing the appearance of Andy McNab, the former SAS soldier and bestselling author who was due to sign his books the following day. As Steve sat and took out his pen a couple approached with a copy of one of Andy McNab's latest blockbusters.

'Could you dedicate it for Wilf and Doris please Andy?' requested the woman.

'I'm not Andy McNab,' she was told.

'Yes you are.'

'No, I'm not.'

'It says' – she pointed to the large poster advertising the visit – Meet Andy McNab– 'you are him.'

'Do I look like Andy McNab?' asked Steve. I am sure my friend will not mind me describing him as somewhat portly in appearance.

'Stop messing about, Andy,' said the woman, thrusting the book in Steve's direction.

'I AM NOT ANDY McNAB!' repeated Steve.

'He's mebbe incognito,' said the woman's companion *sotto voce*. 'For Wilf and Doris, please Andy.'

So my friend duly signed the book: 'Happy Christmas to Wilf and Doris with best wishes Andy McNab.'

I have also had some interesting encounters at book signing events. I signed books along with Ashley Jackson, the artist, at a Christmas literary lunch. Ashley did a little sketch in the front of each book brought to him for dedicating. One woman, on arriving at my table, asked if I would do the same.

'I'm not an artist,' I informed her.

She looked put out. 'Well, Ashley Jackson's done a drawing. Can't you draw a bit of holly and mistletoe?'

After I had obliged, everyone else in the queue demanded the same.

At another event, a man in Leeds stared at me for an inordinate amount of time then at the back of the book where there was a picture of me. 'I'll say one thing,' he remarked, 'you take a good photograph.'

Prior to giving a talk at a festival in Leyburn I waited to sign my books but there were few takers. Then I was approached by a grizzled farmer.

'Are you anybody?' he asked bluntly.

'No,' I replied.

' 'As tha been on owt?'

'No.'

'Is t'book about gardenin'?'

'No.'

'Gardenin' books do very well,' he confided in me.

'Really?'

'What's t'book about, then?'

'It's about my experiences as a school inspector in the Yorkshire Dales – anecdotal and amusing.'

'Dunt sound a barrel of laughs to me,' he said, picking up a copy of my book and scrutinising it.

'Perhaps you would like a copy,' I suggested.

'No, no, not my cup of tea,' he said and then continued. 'Person who was 'ere last year had a gardening book and there was a right old queue out of t'tent and round t'back.'

'Really?'

'Mind you, it were somebody.'

'Who?' I asked.

'Charlie Dimmock.'

'Well, what has he got that I haven't?' I asked mischievously.

'It's a lass and she digs t'garden without a bra.'

'So do I,' I told him.

He laughed. 'Aye, but thas not got what Charlie Dimmock's got.'

I tried to be clever – not a sensible thing with a seasoned Dales' farmer.

'Is that the criterion for writing a book then?' I enquired.

He rubbed his stubble on his chin. ' 'Appen not, but she sold a lot more books than you're likely to do.' And with that he left me to listen to the brass band.

Yorkshire people are known for their bluntness and they do not come blunter than in my home town of Rotherham. It was there I was approached by a woman who informed me that, 'My sister thinks your books are very funny but they don't make me laugh.'

'And a happy Christmas to you,' I said smiling.

4

A CHRISTMAS BABY

BIANCA'S BABY

'Miss, miss!' Chardonnay shouted out and waving her hand in the air, impatient to relate what had happened in her house over the holiday. 'We had a right time at Christmas.'

'Really?' said the teacher.

'Our Bianca had a baby on Christmas Day.'

'Your sister had a baby?'

'Yes miss. On Christmas Day. It were a little boy,' the girl told her, jumping to her feet.

'Well, how old is your sister?'

'Seventeen, miss,' said Chardonnay. 'She didn't know

she was having it and nobody else did either. Mam and dad had gone to the pub in the afternoon and I had to stay in with Bianca because she wasn't feeling too well. Anyway, when my mam and dad had gone out our Bianca said she felt funny and the next thing what happened was she flopped on the settee and all this water come out over the floor and she started moaning and groaning.'

The rest of the class sat in stunned silence during what could only be described as a performance as the girl related the facts in graphic detail and at great speed, illustrating her account with facial expressions and actions. There wasn't a sound. Some children shuffled in embarrassment, others stared at her uncomprehendingly, some pulled faces and others sat open-mouthed. Chardonnay rattled on regardless with ruthless direct-ness and in a voice strong and determined.

'Anyway, I thought she was really ill,' the girl told her audience. 'She kept holding her stomach like this. "Oh!" she went, "I feel awful." Then she told me to go and fetch Dr Stirling but he wasn't in so I went to get Nurse Lloyd who lives on Common Lane. She was a middlewife and used to deliver babies. Anyway she weren't happy having to leave her Christmas tea and told me to go for the

doctor and I told her I had done but he was out. Then she phoned for an ambulance but they said it would be ages coming because of the snow and the roads being icy and all and it being Christmas Day as well so she said she'd come with me. When we got home Bianca was stretched out on the living room floor moaning and groaning and saying she was going to die. Nurse Lloyd looked at her and told me to get some towels and boil some hot water and then she told me to hold Bianca's hand to calm her down because she was moaning and groaning something rotten. Then the baby just popped out. There was lots of blood.' One girl called Chantelle gave an involuntary shudder and there were several sharp intakes of breath. 'I think Mrs Lloyd was mad with the baby because she slapped it on its bum and it started roaring its eyes out. Then this play centre come out.'

'Play centre?' repeated the teacher.

'It's all this gooey stuff what comes out after the baby.'

'Ah, the placenta,' mouthed the teacher.

'And it was fastened to a long sort of cord.'

'What, the play centre?' asked Chantelle, saucer-eyed.

'No it was fastened to the baby. It's called the umbrella cord and Mrs Lloyd had to cut it. She knew what she was doing because she was a middlewife. Mrs Lloyd wrapped the baby in a towel and gave it to our Bianca. Then the ambulance came and I went to fetch my mam and dad from the pub and we all went in to the hospital to see the baby. It was put in an incinerator.' Chardonnay turned to the class. 'If anyone has any questions, I'll answer them.' There was a bewildered silence in the classroom.

'I don't think we'll have questions, thank you Chardonnay,' said the teacher, quite at a loss for what else to say.

'Miss,' said Eddie Lake, 'I got a play centre for Christmas.'

'The doctor's been and everything is fine,' said the sister. 'Mother and baby are doing very well, so you can take them home when you're ready. Now, do try and persevere with the breast-feeding, Mrs Phinn. He's not quite taken to it yet but try and stick at it and he will soon get a taste for it and then there'll be no stopping him.'

Matthew Joseph Phinn, our second child, was our Christmas baby. Unlike his elder brother he was not an enthusiastic breast-feeder but my wife was determined to do as the nurse recommended and not give up.

As Christine was packing the few things she had in her bedside cabinet, I picked the clipboard off the bottom of the bed. The sheet of paper attached to it read 'Doncaster Royal Infirmary/Maternity Unit'. Below was written: **BABY Phinn. WEIGHT: 7lbs 1oz.** Then at the bottom was space for: **DOCTOR'S COMMENT**.

I was removing the sheet of paper when the ward sister came in and caught me red-handed.

'What are you up to?' she asked.

'May I have this, please?'

'No, you may not. It's hospital property.'

'Oh please,' I begged.

'It's more than my job's worth.'

'Please.'

'Why do you want it, anyway?'

'I want to keep it until my son is twenty-one,' I told her seriously, 'and on that special birthday I want to present it to him in a gilt frame and say to him: "When we are dead and gone, perhaps you might sometimes look upon that scrap of paper in the golden frame and remember this very special day, your coming of age, and I hope you might remember a father and a mother who were so very proud of you and loved you more than any other parents loved a son. You see, it's the first thing anybody wrote about you." I shall tell him, "It is the doctor's comment written during your first week of life." You see, sister, that is why I want to keep this sheet of paper.'

'Oh,' said the nurse, who had listened open-mouthed to my commentary. 'How lovely. You're making me cry. And what does the doctor say?'

Smiling, I passed over the piece of paper so she could read what the doctor had written: 'Poor sucker.'

5

FLOWERS FOR CHRISTMAS

CHRISTMAS ROSES

The vicar's wife was walking up the path to the rectory from Morning Service when she caught sight of a small figure placing some flowers on a grave.

'Hello Daniel,' she said.

''Ello miss,' replied the boy.

'You come here quite often don't you?' she said. 'I've seen how well you look after your grandfather's grave. There are always fresh flowers.'

'Aye I do come regular miss.' He pointed to the flowers. 'These are called Christmas roses and they were one of mi granddad's favourite flowers.'

'Actually they are called hellebores and they are amongst my favourites too,' the vicar's wife told him. 'They bloom very early and they like the shade. You could plant some around your grandfather's grave. There's a legend surrounding the hellebores, you know. My husband mentioned it in one of his sermons. When a small girl went to see Baby Jesus in the stable all those years ago she saw that the shepherds and the kings had taken him presents. She had nothing to give and began to weep. The tears fell upon the snow and where they had fallen the hellebore grew and the pure white flowers bloomed. It's a lovely story isn't it?'

Danny was staring up open mouthed. He looked down at the grave, bent and touched the white petals which lay on the top. 'Aye, it is,' he said.

A PRESENT FOR MISS

Thomas was six and it was clear to those who met him that he was a lonely and neglected little boy who desperately sought affection. His shirt was invariably grubby around the collar, his trousers too small for him and his jumper threadbare and stained. The other children in the class kept their distance because he had that unpleasant, unwashed odour about him.

His mother was a sharp-tongued, miserable woman and clearly found it difficult to cope with Thomas and his two younger sisters. Demanding young children, too little money, mounting debts, and an absentee father had taken their toll. It was no surprise that she looked permanently exhausted and that she flew off the handle at every opportunity.

Despite his background, Thomas was a remarkably cheerful little boy who never complained and always tried his limited best at his school work. He loved nothing better that straightening the chairs, giving out the paper and pencils, collecting the books, tidying up the classroom and picking up litter and he took on all these tasks cheerfully, whistling away as if he had not a care in the world.

It was just after the final whole school assembly before the school broke up for Christmas. The children had brought presents and cards for their teacher and gathered around her desk chattering excitedly. Thomas held back until morning break when the other children had left the classroom.

'These are for you, miss,' he said holding up a small bunch of wilting flowers which had seen better days and a sprig of holly with a few berries. Near the school was a cemetery and the teacher had a shrewd idea from where the flowers came.

'They're lovely,' she told him. He nodded and sniffed. 'I shall put them in water and have them on my desk. These shall be my very special flowers.'

'It's not much miss,' said the child sadly.

'It's the thought that counts,' the teacher told him.

The flowers were arranged in a brightly coloured vase and placed in pride of place on the teacher's desk.

'These are my very special flowers, Thomas,' the teacher told him. 'Thank you so much.' Then she whispered, 'I like them better than any other presents I have been given.'

'Miss, where are those dead flowers from?' asked a child later that morning.

The teacher fixed him with one of those looks teachers have perfected over the years, a penetrating look which said 'hold your tongue.'

'They are a present,' she said, 'and they are very special.'

'But miss, they're all dead and—' began the child.

'Enough!' exclaimed the teacher. She could see that Thomas was watching and listening intently. 'Now get on with your work.'

At the end of the day, Thomas appeared at her door.

'Hello, Thomas,' said the teacher brightly. 'Have you come to wish me a Happy Christmas.'

'I've come for my flowers, miss,' he said bluntly.

'Your flowers? Oh, I thought they were for me.'

'They're very special,' the child said solemnly. 'You said they were very special.'

'And they are,' the teacher told him. 'I think they are beautiful but I thought you brought them for me?'

'They're very special,' Thomas repeated, 'and I want to give them to my mam.'

The teacher smiled. 'Of course you do.' She removed the holly, virtually bare of its red berries and the two wilting flowers from the vase and wrapped them in some bright red tissue paper. Then, taking a ribbon from one of the presents, she tied them in a bunch. 'They look really nice now, don't they?' she said. 'What a lovely surprise for your mummy.' She placed the flowers in the child's hands. 'Have a very happy Christmas Thomas,' she said.

Then she watched the boy scurry down the school path to be met at the gates by a stocky, unkempt woman with short bleached hair and a cigarette dangling from her mouth. Two screaming toddlers were writhing and wriggling in the push-chair beside her. On seeing her son, she stabbed the air with a finger and began shouting at him. Reaching her, the little boy held up his bouquet like a priest at the altar making an offering. The flowers were promptly plucked from his hand and deposited in the nearest bin.

6

THE SCHOOL INSPECTOR CALLS!

THE MOST IMPORTANT TIME OF YEAR

There is an old proverb, which goes like this: 'Here's to the child and all he has to teach us.'

I was reminded all too forcefully of this when I visited a Yorkshire primary school in the heart of the Dales. It was there that I met Elizabeth. She was a tall girl of about eleven, with pink-framed glasses and a rather earnest expression.

'Are you looking forward to Christmas?' I realised it was a rather inane question which I asked her but she answered pleasantly and with a small smile.

'Oh yes, it's a lovely time of year,' she said. 'I love the

smells of mince pies and fir trees and all the lights twink-ling. And I like the Christmas morning service, the carols and the readings. The church is always full and everyone is friendly and happy.'

'Well, Christmas is the most important time in the Christian year, isn't it?' I said casually.

'No,' she replied. 'I don't think you will find it is.'

'Pardon?'

'I said, no, it isn't. Christmas is not the most important time in the Christian year.'

'Oh.' I was quite taken aback.

'It's Easter, Mr Phinn,' she told me. 'That's when Jesus suffered on the cross, died for our sins and rose from the dead.'

'Yes, of course,' I said hurriedly. 'The only one to do so.'

'What?'

'Rise from the dead.'

'No, that's not right either.' Oh dear, I thought. A walking biblical encyclopaedia. 'There was Mary and Martha's brother.'

'Who?'

'Lazarus.'

'Oh, yes,' I said. 'I'd forgotten about Lazarus.'

'And don't forget Jairus's daughter. Jesus told him that she wasn't dead but sleeping and said, "Little maid, arise."'

'Oh yes, of course. How could I have forgotten Jairus's daughter.'

'Mr Phinn,' said the girl, scrutinising me through the pink frames of her spectacles, 'your biblical knowledge is not all that good, is it?'

A VISIT TO THE HEAD TEACHER

The interior of the school was warm and welcoming. A tall Christmas tree stood in one corner of the classroom, festooned with coloured lights and decorations; a large rustic crib was set in the opposite corner. Every wall was covered with children's Christmas paintings in reds and greens and golds. There were snowmen and reindeer, plum puddings and fir trees, Father Christmases and carol singers and some delightful silhouettes showing the journey of Mary and Joseph to Bethlehem.

After a tour of the building, I joined the head teacher in his room. I was there to attend his leaving assembly.

'This must be a bit of an emotional time for you,' I said, sitting in a chair opposite his desk.

He sighed. 'Yes indeed. I've been a teacher for forty years and a head teacher for thirty. I shall be very sorry to leave but I think it's about time I retired. There's a special assembly for me this afternoon and the teachers have told me that I have to make myself scarce. That's why I'm closeted in my room. I reckon I'll have a job getting through the assembly without a few tears.' He leaned back in his chair. 'I've loved this job,' he said. 'Not all of the time of course, but most of it. I could have done without the paper-work and league tables and targets, the guidelines and government directives which come over the Dales like the plagues of Egypt.' He gave a small smile. 'And the school inspections,' he added. 'I shall miss the children the most.'

There was a knock at the door.

'Come in!' shouted the head teacher.

A boy of about ten or eleven entered. He had curly blond hair, clear blue eyes and a face full of freckles.

'Oh dear,' sighed the head teacher shaking his head. 'It's you Dean. I didn't think it would be too long before you made an appearance in my room.'

'Sir—' began the boy.

'One moment!' snapped the head teacher holding up his hand as if stopping traffic. He turned to me. 'Do you know, Mr Phinn, this young man spends more time in my room than he does in his classroom.'

'Sir, I just—' started the boy again.

'One moment,' interrupted the head teacher. He turned to me again. 'I am afraid that Dean here seems to attract trouble like a magnet.'

'But sir—'

'He is forever in my room for one thing or another. How many times did Mrs Pick send you to me last week?'

'It was twice sir, but—'

'Twice in one week,' said the head teacher shaking his head again. 'And you always have some wild and wonderful excuse. "I didn't mean to hit him, I didn't mean to break it, I didn't mean to call her those names, I didn't mean to use those naughty words." You never mean to Dean, but you always seem to do it, don't you?'

The boy's eyes brimmed with tears and his bottom lip began to tremble.

'And however many times I tell you to behave yourself you still manage to get into some sort of trouble.'

The boy looked up, wiped away his tears with a grubby fist and sniffed noisily. 'This is Mr Phinn and he is a very, very important person,' the head teacher told him. 'Mr Phinn is a school inspector.' The boy stared at me like a frightened animal in the headlights' glare. 'And when Mr Phinn came into our school this morning, he said what a lovely school – bright and cheerful and welcoming with cushions in the Reading Corner and pictures, double-mounted, on the walls and wonderful displays down the corridor. I wonder what Mr Phinn is thinking now.'

'I don't know, sir,' muttered the child.

'No, neither do I,' said the head teacher. 'You know I am retiring at the end of this week?'

'Yes sir.'

'I was telling Mr Phinn that I shall miss a lot about the school and particularly the children but I have to tell you this Dean, I will not miss you being sent to my room every week for getting into trouble.'

The boy looked down.

'Now then,' continued the head teacher, 'what is it this time. Why are you in my room again?'

Dean dug into his pocket and produced a white envelope. 'I just came to give you this card sir,' said the boy, 'and to wish you a happy retirement and a merry Christmas.'

TEQUILA'S BOBBLES

I called in at Crompton Primary School just prior to the school breaking up for the Christmas holidays. Mrs Gardiner's room was so crammed full of brightly-wrapped Christmas packages that there was hardly any room for me to get in.

'Sorry about this, Mr Phinn,' apologised the head teacher, clambering around the piles of boxes. 'We don't want the children to see them and my room is the safest place.'

'Are these all for the children?' I asked, amazed by the spectacle before me.

'Indeed, they are,' the head teacher replied. 'We like to give each child a small gift at Christmas. Always a book. Nursery rhymes or fairy tales for the infants, a poetry anthology or children's novel for the older ones.'

'What a lovely idea,' I said. 'But however can you afford it?'

'Well, the Rotary Club and the Lions help out,' explained Mrs Gardiner, 'and we have raffles during the year, bingo sessions and other fund-raising activities. It raises just about enough. You see, some of our children might have wonderful televisions at home and video games and PlayStations but no books at all, not one. They get lots of toys and sweets and bicycles on Christmas morning but seldom a book. They never visit the library and are rarely seen in a bookshop. So I think it's important for them to have a reading book. Then there are other children in the school who will get precious little at all for Christmas. Our book might be one of the few things they do get. We once had one little boy whose mother told him that Father Christmas had run out of presents when he got to him. Sad, isn't it?'

'It is,' I agreed. 'You're passionate about reading, aren't you, Mrs Gardiner?'

'Yes, I suppose I am,' she replied. 'I always have been. I get it from my parents. My father used to say that books are the architecture of a civilised society and reading the most important tool of learning.'

'He was a wise man,' I said.

'Taught for forty years, did my father,' said Mrs Gardiner proudly. 'My mother read to me every night until I was well into my teens, and she bought me a book every birthday and every Christmas and always inscribed it with a little message. Those books are my treasured possessions. I remember when I first became head teacher here at Crompton and asked a child what books he had at home. I have to admit I was shocked by the answer. After thinking a bit, he replied that they did have one – a big, thick, yellow book which they kept underneath the telephone. I feel that children should own books and build up a little personal library, so we buy them one each Christmas and put a bookplate in the front with their name and the date. Reading is so important. If parents would just spend fifteen minutes each evening with their children, talking about the words and the pictures and making reading enjoyable, what a difference it would make to their learning.'

'I couldn't agree more,' I told her.

'And do you know, some of the children are coming into this school at five having never had a story read to them at bedtime or heard a nursery rhyme. Some parents just don't seem to bother these days. The children know all the pop song lyrics, of course, but few of the traditional rhymes. We have to teach them about Jack and Jill and Humpty Dumpty and Little Jack Horner.'

'Well, I think it's a splendid idea to buy the children books, I really do.'

'There's only one problem,' said the head teacher.

'Oh?'

'Father Christmas.'

'Why?' I asked. 'What has Father Christmas done?'

'He hasn't done anything,' said Mrs Gardiner. 'It's just that we haven't got one. The crossing patrol warden took on the part last year but ended up nearly having a nervous breakdown. He said he'd rather face a roadful of careering traffic than the hall full of excited children again. I have to say they did give him a bit of a hard time. Tequila interrogated him as to why she hadn't received the presents she had asked for the previous year, another child told him he wasn't the real Father Christmas and one little girl got completely carried away, fastened onto him like a Whitby limpet and just would not let go. She screamed and yelled and when we finally managed to prise her off she threw a most disgraceful tantrum. Then Father Christmas's beard kept slipping and he forgot the names of the reindeers.'

'I can certainly sympathise,' I told her, recalling my disastrous attempt at being Santa Claus. 'I too have had similar experiences when I played Father Christmas.'

The head teacher paused for a moment and gave me a sly sort of look. 'So, you have played Father Christmas, have you?' she said.

'Yes but—' I began.

'Now, I've just had a thought. Mr Phinn. You don't fancy—'

I cut her off, throwing up my hands as though to fend her off. 'No, no, Mrs Gardiner, I've played Father Christmas before and it is not false modesty when I tell you that I was an unmitigated disaster.'

'Ah well,' she said, 'I shall just have to twist my husband's arm.' At that moment there was a loud rap on the door. 'Excuse me, Mr Phinn,' said the head teacher.

Outside she was confronted by a round, shapeless woman with bright frizzy blonde hair, an impressive set of double chins and immense hips. She had a ruddy complexion, heavy sleepy eyes and a mouth which turned downwards as if in perpetual hostility.

'Can I 'ave a word, Mrs Gardiner,' she said angrily.

'I am a little busy at the minute, Mrs Braithwaite,' replied the head teacher.

'Yes, well you might be, but this is important.'

'It always is, Mrs Braithwaite,' sighed Mrs Gardiner.

'Eh?'

'What seems to be the problem this time?'

'Our Tequila came 'ome yesterday wi'out 'er Christmas bobbles. She had 'em in 'er 'air yesterday morning when she come to school and she come 'ome wi'out 'em. Somebody's gone an' nicked 'em off of 'er.'

'We can't be certain about that,' replied the head teacher. 'They might have fallen out when she was running around in the playground.'

'No, they didn't!' snapped Tequila's mother. 'I tied 'em on right tight. She come 'ome wi'out 'em, rooarin' 'er eyes out. They was new, them bobbles. Just bought 'em from t'market.'

'And what do these Christmas bobbles look like?' enquired Mrs Gardiner.

'Well, they was red Father Christmases wi' winking eyes. I didn't shell out good money to 'ave 'em nicked.'

'We will have a good look round for them, Mrs Braithwaite, and now if you will excuse me, I am rather busy.'

'No!' cried Tequila's mother. 'That won't do. It won't do at all. Somebody's nicked 'er bobbles and I want 'em findin'. It's 'appened before. My Tequila's come 'ome without other things which 'ave gone missing – like her Mickey Mouse knickers for one thing.'

'Mrs Braithwaite,' said the head teacher sharply. 'Leave the matter with me and I will make inquiries. Now I really must ask you—'

The woman was not to be put off. 'Well, I want to know what you are going to do.'

'Well, let me see,' said Mrs Gardiner calmly. 'Tomorrow, I shall get the teachers, the classroom assistants, the dinner ladies, the mid-day supervisors, the cleaners, the lollipop lady, the caretaker and all the children to search for Tequila's Christmas bobbles which must have cost you all of two pounds. We will stop all the lessons to look high and low and we will leave no stone unturned until we have found them.'

Mrs Braithwaite paused for a moment before replying, 'I should bloody well think so,' oblivious of the sarcasm. She then marched out of the room.

Mrs Gardiner informed me that it was an uphill battle trying to get the children not to fight and swear.

'Of course,' she told me, 'much of the bad language emanates at home where the children hear their parents swear and see them sometimes being violent.'

She recounted how on one occasion she had spoken of her concerns to a parent at the gates of the school complaining about her son swearing and fighting.

'Well I don't know where he gets it from,' replied the disgruntled mother.

'Will you have a word with him please?' asked the head teacher.

'I'll do more than that,' said the parent, 'Little bugger! I'll tan his little arse for him.'

O HOLY NIGHT

Two weeks before the Christmas holidays a team of three school inspectors arrived at the secondary school. The visit, termed 'a dip stick' inspection, was to last for only two days, the focus being the core subjects of English, Mathematics and Science. The lead inspector, a large, amiable and avuncular figure was asked by the head teacher if he might include an inspection of the music in the school. She explained that Mr Morgan, the head of the department, was to retire at the end of term after thirty five years of dedicated teaching and he was keen that his work should be seen by an inspector.

'In all the years he has been teaching,' explained the head teacher, 'he has never been inspected. He is such an enthusiastic and committed teacher; it would be so good for him to leave on a high with an endorsement of his excellent work by a school inspector.' She was confident that the music department, which she described as the jewel in the crown, would emerge with flying colours. The lead inspector explained that there was no inspector on the team qualified to inspect music; their specialisms were English, Mathematics and Science. The head teacher persisted so it came about that I was dragooned into observing Mr Morgan's lessons.

The head of music was delighted to see me when I arrived at his classroom and warmly shook my hand.

'And what instrument do you play?' he asked.

'The piano,' I replied. I did not reveal that my playing was indifferent at best.

'Fabulous!' he exclaimed, patting me on the back. 'You can accompany the choir. Miss Smithers is off with the flu.' He smiled widely. 'You're heaven sent.'

'I'm not sure about that,' I began.

'It's only the one carol we have to practise,' he told me. 'O Holy Night. Very easy accompaniment in the key of C. You'll have no trouble, no trouble at all.'

I felt my heart begin to beat in my chest.

However, I managed to cope reasonably well. The children sang with gusto and one young man sang the solo part beautifully.

It was clear that Mr Morgan was indeed an outstanding teacher and I had no hesitation in giving him an excellent report.

The team of inspectors was invited by the head teacher to attend the carol concert planned for that evening. Fortunately for me, Miss Smithers, sniffing and snuffling into her handkerchief left her bed to accompany the choir so I was not called upon to repeat my performance on the piano.

The choir began to sing:

O holy night! The stars are brightly shining,
It is the night of our dear Saviour's birth.
Long lay the world in sin and error pining.
Till He appeared and the Spirit felt its worth.
A thrill of hope, the weary world rejoices,
For yonder breaks a new and glorious morn.

Then the young soloist sang. His clear, high, perfectly-pitched singing filled the hushed hall. It was a heavenly voice.

Fall on your knees! Oh, hear the angel voices!
O night divine, the night when Christ was born;
O night. O holy night . . .

And when he reached the very top note the boy's voice suddenly cracked and he emitted a dreadful squawking sound. It was the very worst time for his voice to break. He looked distraught and on the verge of tears. Then something very special happened. The choir gathered around and two boys put their hands on his shoulders and they took up the tune.

O night divine!
O night, O holy night, O night divine!

There was not a dry eye in the hall.

7

A CHRISTMAS CAROL

WHAT THE DICKENS?

I was privileged to meet and to hear the great, great, great granddaughter of Charles Dickens who was giving a series of lectures on the works of her famous forebear. In one memorable lecture Lucinda Dickens-Hawksley gave a fascinating commentary on a story which is quintessentially Dickens: *A Christmas Carol*. This little book, which appeared in 1853 is, in essence, symbolic of everything the great novelist held most dear. At one level the novel has influenced much of what we associate with Christmas: roast turkey and plum pudding, mince pies and spiced punch, blazing log fires and wreathes of holly, a time of festive generosity and good cheer. This idealisation of Christmas is foreshadowed by Dickens in *The Pickwick Papers* which appeared in 1837. On a much deeper level however *A Christmas Carol*, far from being a celebration of the revelry and plenty at Christmas, is a dark and disturbing story and a powerful appeal for greater charity and compassion in the world.

Having read and been appalled by the Parliamentary Report on *The Employment and Condition of Children in Mines and Manufactories* of 1842 with its dreadful descriptions of undernourished and sick children condemned to work underground for ten hours at a time, Dickens decided to write a polemical pamphlet entitled *An Appeal to the People of England on Behalf of the Poor Man's Child.* In a powerful fund-raising speech for the relief of the poor at the Manchester Athenaeum Institute, he told his audience:

My own heart dies within me when I see thousands of immortal creatures condemned without alternative or choice, not to what our great poet calls 'the primrose path to the everlasting bonfire' but one of jagged flints and stones, laid down by brutal ignorance.

Having thought long and hard, Dickens decided that instead of a pamphlet a story would be a more effective means of communicating his message and have greater impact on the general public. He would appeal to the heart and not the head. So Dickens began *A Christmas Carol*, completing most of the book in just six weeks.

In an inner-city comprehensive the school play was an adaptation of *A Christmas Carol*. The stage sets were very basic, the costumes rather shabby and ill-fitting and much of the acting was wooden and yet the production made a powerful impression on those of us in the audience.

When the Ghost of Christmas Present leaves, the cowering Scrooge, with his pinched nose, thin lips and shrivelled cheeks, has to face the most frightening spectre of all – The Ghost of Christmas Yet to Come.

'I see something strange and not belonging to yourself,' says the trembling miser. 'Is it a foot or a claw?'

'It might be a claw for the flesh there is upon it,'

replies the spirit, revealing two small and emaciated children from beneath the folds of his robe.

'Spirit, are they yours?' asks Scrooge.

'They are Man's,' the spectre tells him. 'This boy is Ignorance. This girl is Want. Beware them both but most of all beware the boy for on his brow I see that written which is Doom unless the writing be erased.'

In the end Scrooge learns compassion in a dramatic change of heart.

'I am not the man I was,' he tells the spirit. 'I will honour Christmas in my heart and try to keep it all the year.' He becomes determined to live a new life, a life not ruled by money and greed but one where his heart is opened to those in need.

Leaving the school on that frosty evening following the production, we had been reminded of the real meaning of Christmas – a time of kindness and compassion.

8

THE PANTOMIME

A CHILDHOOD MEMORY

Every Christmas my father would take me to the pantomime. I loved the pantomimes with their simple plots
where good always triumphed, the outrageous cross-
dressing characters, the doggerel, the ridiculously silly
jokes and play on words, the foolish antics, the bright
colours, the spectacularly gaudy costumes, the lively
music and the audience participation where you were
encouraged to shout out as loud as you could. It is a
remarkable fact that the pantomime has survived to the
present day and is as popular as ever despite competition
from television, videos, DVDs, blockbuster movies and

sophisticated computer games. Everything about this over-the-top theatrical genre appeals to children and when things go wrong, which they frequently do, this is an added bonus.

I was never frightened by the wicked witch or the cruel stepmother, the villainous King Rat or the scheming Sheriff of Nottingham because I had met these characters in the stories my parents had read to me and I knew in my heart that they would eventually get their come-uppance. It was great fun, however, watching screaming children, terrified by the 'baddie', being hauled from their seats and taken out by their embarrassed parents.

It is an old theatrical chestnut; 'Never act with animals or children.' Both are, of course, entirely unpredictable. Once, so my father reminded me (although I have to admit I cannot remember, so it might be one of his tall tales) the Shetland pony harnessed to Cinderella's crystal coach (a large, round pumpkin-shaped cardboard cut-out) made an appearance on stage amidst delighted '*OOOOs*' and '*Aaaaaahhhhhs*' from the audience. Just as Cinderella emerged from her magical carriage in her shimmering silver dress and sparkling glass slippers, the pony decided it was a good time to relieve itself. The contents of the creature's bladder splashed onto the floor and then trickled across the stage, into the orchestra pit and onto the piano much to the alarm of the pianist and the amusement of the audience and the actors. Buttons, with great presence of mind, disappeared and returned a moment later with a mop and the lines:

Goodness gracious, dearie me
Cinder's pony's done a wee

I do remember, however, the time when Buttons tried his hardest to get a little boy who sat in the middle of the front row to respond. We were at the end of the row so had a clear view. The six year old stared at the action on stage with a deadpan expression, refusing when everyone else was cheering and booing, shouting and singing. Every actor tried to get the child to react – Cinderella, the Fairy Godmother, the Wicked Stepmother, the Ugly Sisters, Baron Hardup – all to no avail. Buttons saw this as a personal challenge. He would run onto the stage with 'Hi Kids!' and all the children would shout back 'Hi Buttons!'. All, that is, except the child sitting in the middle of the front row with the impassive expression. Buttons began to look pointedly at the child.

'I get really upset if children don't say "Hi Buttons",' he said sadly.

'Aaaaahhhh,' commiserated the audience.

'And there's a little boy on the front row who hasn't said it yet.'

'Aaaaahhhh,' chorused the audience again.

Still there was no response from the child so Buttons left the stage, skipped down the steps leading to the auditorium and, taking the child's hand managed to prevail upon him to join him on stage with a promise of a present.

'Now little boy,' he asked, 'what's your name?' The child stared at him in silence.

Buttons tried another tack. 'Are you having a good time?' Still there was no response. Buttons persevered. 'Have you anything to say to Buttons?' The little boy looked up and replied in a dead-pan voice, 'Does tha know summat, tha bloody daft thee' and returned to his seat.

On another occasion Simple Simon asked for some children to join him on stage. From the sea of waving hands he selected an angelic-looking little boy of about six. The child duly joined the actor on stage and was given the microphone.

'You entertain the audience while I am gone,' Simple Simon told the child.

The idea was that the child, standing in the centre of the stage nervous and alone and not knowing what to do, would generate a deal of laughter from the audience as he looked around nervously. Simple Simon had picked the wrong child. The little boy, not at all disconcerted by the full theatre, suddenly went into a stage act to rival the best stand-up comedian and much to the delight of a very appreciative audience.

'I say, I say, I say,' began the child, 'I got an empty box last Christmas. My dad said it was an Action Man Deserter kit. My dad treated my mum to plastic surgery this year for Christmas. He cut up her credit card,' There was a great round of applause. The boy continued. 'I told my dad I had my eye on a bike for Christmas. He told me to keep my eye on it because I wasn't going to get my bum on it.' A flustered Simple Simon reappeared on the stage and grabbed the microphone from the budding comedian.

'Thank you very much little boy,' he said, laughing half-heartedly.

'I've not finished,' protested the child, attempting to get back possession of the microphone.

'Oh, yes you have,' said Simple Simon, escorting him off the stage.

'Oh, no he hasn't!' chorused the audience.

My father told me of another occasion when the actor playing the pantomime Dame collapsed in the interval and had to be taken to Moorgate Hospital. The theatre manager appeared before the curtain prior to the commencement of the second act to announce: 'The actor playing the part of Dame Trot will not be appearing in the second half. He's been taken ill.'

The audience in one great chorus shouted: 'Oh no, he hasn't!'

'Yes, yes he has,' replied the manager in all seriousness.

'Oh no, he hasn't!' the audience shouted back.

'Oh yes, he has!' shouted the manager angrily.

One afternoon just before Christmas when I was ten my father took me to see the pantomime at the Leeds City Varieties. We caught the train from Masborough

Station and walked through the city crowded with shoppers. It was one of the few very special occasions when it was just me and my Dad, no brothers or sister. The City Varieties is the oldest extant music hall in the country, an intimate, colourful and atmospheric little theatre, hidden between two arcades. All the greats of variety theatre have performed here: Charlie Chaplin and Houdini, Tommy Cooper and Hylda Baker, Marie Lloyd and Les Dawson and, of course, the legendary Ken Dodd who took some persuading to leave the stage once he'd started. I appeared on stage there myself in 2006 in my one-man-show and spent the intermission leafing through the visitors' book fascinated by the many entries. Before my performance I stood on the empty stage looking down at the empty stalls and recalled a small boy sitting on a plush red velvet seat with his father, his eyes (as we say in Yorkshire) 'like chapel hat pegs', entering a magical world of the pantomime.

A VISIT TO THE PANTOMIME

Every year at Christmas time
Dad takes me to the pantomime,
Where raucous children dream and shout
And clap and cheer and jump about.
The noise, it drives me quite insane,
And every year it is the same.
When I see Cinders and the Prince
I sit and sulk and scowl and wince.
The ugly sisters are inane
And there's nothing funny about the Dame.
I shake my head and moan and groan
And beg that I be taken home.
It's childish but I have to go
Because my father loves it so.

THE FAIRY QUEEN

My father, a great storyteller, rarely told me of the time he was in the army during the War but he once told me the story (I was grown up at the time) that he had heard when serving in North Africa. An ENSA group arrived one Christmas to entertain the troops (several hundred tough Seaforth Highlanders) with a spoof version of the pantomime 'Cinderella'. All the parts, including the female ones were taken by serving soldiers. The Fairy Queen in the pantomime was played by a large red-haired Scot who clearly had a wry sense of humour for he appeared on stage dressed for the part in white taffeta and a tiara shouting out the lines:

Oh I am the Fairy Queen,
Of whom you are so fond,
Please tell me, tell me, tell me please,
Where shall I put my wand?

Foreseeing the predictable answer from the troops the RSM leapt to his feet and bawled, 'First man who speaks, seven days confined to barracks!'

9

A CHRISTMAS GIFT

A SHORT STORY

Miss O'Malley felt cold. It was a raw morning and she rarely ventured out on such a bitter day but 'needs must' as she told herself. She examined the display in the window of Archer's Antiques. Well, it wasn't really an antique shop but more of a pawnbroker's and the 'display' was a jumble of miscellaneous objects: a few chipped china figurines, a tarnished trumpet, a battered leather case with faded gold initials on the front, an old record player, various wooden boxes, a cabinet full of cheap-looking jewellery, a couple of pewter tankards and a pile of dusty books. What caught Miss O'Malley's eye was the picture of the Virgin and Child which rested on a rusty tin helmet. It was an unusual depiction, dark and atmospheric, unlike the garish over-sentimental representation of the gentle-faced Mary draped in pale blue and with a golden halo, pictures which were on the front of so many Christmas cards. This Mary clutched her baby protectively to her breast and had a sad faraway look in her eyes as if she could foresee the terrible fate which awaited her son. The baby was different too. Here was no plump rosy-cheeked happy little child; Baby Jesus looked tetchy. But there was something about the painting which Miss O'Malley liked. It was unusual and she liked unusual things. Of course, she was not there to buy, she was there to sell.

Miss O'Malley hovered indecisively for a moment in the shop doorway before entering. The bell tinkled. Behind the counter, leaning on his elbows and reading a newspaper, was a large bald-headed man with a round fleshy face and eyebrows which curled like question marks. He raised his face and stared at her with sunken eyes, grey and watery like that of a fish.

'Now then, my dear,' he said, smiling, 'what can I do for you?'

'I've something to sell,' replied Miss O'Malley.

'Well, that's what I'm here for, to buy and sell. What have you got for me, darling?'

The old woman rummaged inside the canvas shopping bag until she found the round metal tin. On the front was a faded portrait of the young Queen Elizabeth in her coronation robes.

'It's some jewellery,' said Miss O'Malley, passing the tin over the counter. 'I never wear it. It's stuck in a dresser. I've not any use for it now.' She smiled. 'There's not much call for somebody my age to get dressed up these days.'

'Well let's see what we've got, shall we?' said the shopkeeper, emptying out the contents of the tin onto the counter. He poked the rings and lockets with apparent disinterest. There was a delicate pendant of peridots and seed pearls, an ornate fob with an agate stone, a red gold bracelet and various rings and a heavy silver chain. *Quite a little treasure trove*, he thought. He could get a good price for this little lot. He reached for a small eyeglass and examined the jewellery more closely. Then, shaking his head theatrically he sucked in his breath between his teeth.

'Some pretty things here,' he told the woman, casually, 'but nothing of any great value.'

'Oh,' said Miss O'Malley, 'I thought perhaps there was something of worth there.'

'I'm not saying it's worthless, my dear, it's just that this sort of thing doesn't fetch a lot to tell you the truth. There's not much call for this sort of stuff these days.' He held up the delicate peridot pendant with its filigree setting and intricate workmanship. 'People don't wear this sort of jewellery any more. Old fashioned you see. They want bling.'

'Bling?'

'Modern stuff. Heavy gold chains and thick brace-lets.'

'Some of it is gold,' said Miss O'Malley.

'Oh yes, love, there's some gold here. Not the best quality but gold all the same. What they do with stuff like this is melt it down. Old gold you see. I'll take it off your hands but I can't promise I can give you a good price for it. Most of it'll probably go for scrap.'

'The jewellery was my mother's,' replied the old woman, twisting a ring around her finger. 'The silver chain was my father's. I shouldn't like to think they would be melted down.'

'I dare say someone might like some of this stuff as it is,'

said the pawnbroker, 'but it's not most people's cup of tea.'
Miss O'Malley stood there for a moment. 'Look, love,' said
the shopkeeper, putting the jewellery back in the tin box and
pushing it across the counter. 'I'd keep it, if I was you. You
don't want to get rid of your mother's jewellery.' He looked
down at his paper and pretended to read, knowing the
woman would eventually sell. She was dressed in a threadbare coat and old boots and from the way she stood there
with her battered canvas shopping bag hanging loosely from
her arm, he could tell that she clearly needed the money.

'How much do you think you might give me for the
jewellery?' she asked.

The pawnbroker looked up and rubbed his chin.
'Hundred and fifty quid. How does that suit you?'

'I was expecting a little more?' said the woman.

'That's what they all say love,' he told her. 'I'd like to
give you more, I really would, but times are hard and like
everyone else, I've got to make a living and, as I said,
there not much call for this sort of thing these days. I
mean people don't wear watch chains any more. They
want fancy wristwatches. Hundred and sixty. I can't be
fairer than that and I'm being generous giving you that
much.'

'Perhaps a little more,' said the woman.

The man smiled and pointed a finger across the corner. 'You drive a hard bargain, love. Hundred and seventy then. And that's my final offer.'

'I shall have to think about it,' she said.

'You do that, love,' said the pawnbroker. 'I'm not going anywhere.' He looked down at the newspaper again but raised his face when the woman didn't move.

'Was there something else, love?'

'I like the picture in the window,' said the woman.

'Which is that?'

'The Madonna and Child.'

'The what?'

'The Virgin and Child. The one painted on wood.'

'Oh yes, nice little picture is that. Got it from a house clearance on Richard Road. Woman what died was very religious. Had a house full of statues and pictures of Jesus and saints and I don't know what. Daughter wasn't that way inclined and just wanted some of the furniture and the jewellery but wanted rid of most of the stuff.'

'It's very unusual.'

'Not really, love. People aren't very religious these days and there's not that much call for all that stuff.'

'No, I meant the picture. It's very unusual.'

'Well, if you like it, I can give you a very good price.'

'What would you want for it?' asked Miss O'Malley.

'Look, love, I'll tell you what I'll do,' said the pawn-broker. 'Being Christmas, I'm feeling generous. Hundred and seventy quid for the jewellery and I'll throw in the picture. How about that?'

Miss O'Malley nodded. 'Yes, that will be fine.'

Father Dolan, standing with his back to the small one-bar electric fire in Miss O'Malley's sitting room, rubbed his large hands together vigorously. The room was dim and musty with dark heavy furniture, a well-worn brown carpet and faded green curtains.

'It's very cold in here,' he observed.

'It is, Father,' agreed his parishioner. 'I don't have the heating on all day, you see.'

'You really must look after yourself, Miss O'Malley,' he told her, his face soft with concern. 'We don't want you getting hypothermia. You must keep yourself warm in this weather. It's bitter outside this afternoon.'

'Heating is so very expensive,' said the old lady.

'It is,' agreed the priest, sighing and reaching into the pocket of his overcoat for his gloves. 'My congregation at St Mary's are forever complaining about the cold church. We need a whole new boiler I'm afraid. But, it's very important that you keep warm.'

'God will provide, father,' Miss O'Malley told him. 'That's what my mother always used to say.'

The priest smiled and pulled on his gloves and shivered. 'Yes indeed,' he said thinking that it would be a good thing if the good Lord did something about the state of His church. There was the leaking roof, the damp on the wall in the Lady Altar and, of course, the ancient and ineffective heating system.

'I remember last year when you wanted some fresh straw for the crib in the church,' Miss O'Malley reminded him.

'Ah yes,' chuckled the priest, recalling the previous Christmas.

'And you said a prayer and—'

'Coming out of the church a passing tractor loaded with hay caught its tyre on the pavement and shed a bale right before my very eyes.' Father Dolan shook his head and smiled again. 'I don't think, however, that a new heating system will drop off the back of a lorry, but one never knows.'

'God moves in mysterious ways, father,' added Miss O'Malley. 'That's another thing my mother always used to say.'

'Indeed,' agreed the priest. 'Well, let us hope our prayers will be answered this time.'

As Mrs O'Malley was putting on the kettle the priest noticed the painting propped up on the old dresser.

'What's this?' he asked as she appeared from the kitchen and placed a tray with cups and saucers on the table.

'It's the painting I bought today from Archer's Antiques,' she told him. 'It's unusual isn't it?'

'It is,' agreed the priest. 'Rather dark and depressing. I can't say that I've ever seen a painting of the Nativity quite like this. They are usually so bright and cheerful.'

'That's what I told Mr Archer,' said Miss O'Malley. 'In all the pictures on the Christmas cards Mary sits there in her blue cloak and with her golden halo like a queen, smiling away without a spot on her and little Baby Jesus on her lap with hardly a stitch of clothing on. There are the kings in all their fancy finery and Joseph looking clean as a whistle. Even the shepherds look scrubbed. I reckon it wouldn't have been a bit like that, not in a dirty old stable on a cold winter's night. I think it would have looked more like the scene in my picture.'

'You may very well be right,' said the priest. He leaned closer to examine the painting. 'It's very old,' he said. 'I recall seeing something like this when I was in Florence in a small out-of-the-way church. I think it may have been part of an altar piece. That would explain why it is painted on wood rather than canvas and has no frame. I wonder Miss O'Malley, if I might show this to Mrs Charlesworth. She's the Head of the Art Department at St Dominic's and might know something about it. One never knows, it could be worth something.'

'I wouldn't want to sell it, father,' said Miss O'Malley. 'I've taken quite a shine to it. But you can show Mrs Charlesworth by all means. I'd be interested to know something about it.'

Father Dolan called the following week.

'I may have some very good news for you, Miss O'Malley,' he told her, rubbing his large hands together. 'Mrs Charlesworth was very taken with the painting. It is, as I thought, very old and it might be quite rare. She thinks it may be part of something called a triptych and that it could be quite valuable.'

'Good gracious me!' exclaimed Miss O'Malley. 'An old painting like that. Fancy.'

'Indeed,' said the priest enthusiastically. 'It would probably have been the central piece of a three-panelled altar piece. Actually I've seen quite a few of these and, after talking to Mrs Charlesworth, I have done a bit of research. The middle part usually depicts the main focus of the painting, in this case the Holy Family. The two wings or shutters would have probably depicted the shepherds on one side and the Magi in the other. Evidently the smaller triptychs were for domestic devotion but the larger ones, like the one I saw in the church in Florence, would have been in pride of place in the church. The two wings of this triptych are probably lost but Mrs Charlesworth still thinks this might be worth quite a deal of money.'

'I don't know what to say,' said Miss O'Malley. 'One wonders how it ended up in Mr Archer's antique shop.'

'Well, in the last century,' the priest told her, 'the rich aristocrats often visited Europe as part of what was called 'The Grand Tour' and picked up quite a lot of art work and artefacts particularly from Italy. It was quite common evidently for statues and pictures taken from old churches to be bought as souvenirs and end up in this country. Mrs Charlesworth thinks this is the case here, that some nobleman or other bought it and brought it back. It is admittedly not the most attractive representation of the Madonna and Child and was probably passed down to someone who didn't like it and wasn't aware of its value. I don't wish to raise your hopes, but I think perhaps you maybe have a treasure here.'

'Who would have thought it,' murmured Miss O'Malley, shaking her head.

'Mrs Charlesworth is in London next week,' continued Father Dolan, 'and asked if she might take the painting along to Sotheby's, that's the big auction house, and get a valuation.'

'Well, yes,' said Miss O'Malley. 'I would like to know more about it.'

'And how much it is worth,' added the priest.

Miss O'Malley was lighting a candle in the Lady

Chapel at St Mary's when Father Dolan came out of the presbytery.

'Hello Miss O'Malley,' he said cheerfully. 'I thought it was you.'

'Oh hello, Father, I'm just lighting a candle to give thanks,' said the old woman.

'Some good news?'

'Oh yes, Father, some very good news. I'm coming into some money. Quite a lot of money in fact. I shall now be able to pay for your roof and your boiler and not go short myself. God has provided, as I guessed he would. I shall be very comfortably off.'

'Ah,' sighed the priest nodding, 'I guessed as much. Mrs Charlesworth's been in touch, I take it?'

'Oh yes,' sad Miss O'Malley, 'she called around earlier in the week.'

'And she brought news of the painting she took to Sotheby's, I assume?'

'She did Father, yes.'

'You know, when I first saw the painting I knew it was very old and probably of some value. It was a most unusual picture and I guess it will fetch a substantial sum at auction.'

'I doubt that very much, Father,' Miss O'Malley told him, smiling.

'Oh, I think you'll be surprised.'

'I'll be very surprised, Father,' she told the priest, 'because it's not worth the wood it's painted on.'

'I beg your pardon?' asked the priest.

'It's a fake, an imitation of some famous painting or other. Mrs Charlesworth told me that the man at Sotheby's said it was a poor quality reproduction, quite worthless. Evidently, a lot of these rich aristocrats who travelled around Europe in the last century with more money than sense were sold cheap copies thinking they were the genuine articles and this is one of them.'

'But the money!' cried Father Dolan. 'You said you were coming into a great deal of money.'

'And so I am,' said Miss O'Malley. 'I've won the lottery.'

IO

CRUISING AT CHRISTMAS

A SHORT STORY

'So have you been on a cruise before?' The speaker was a large, red-faced individual with the staring eyes of a deep-sea fish. He looked as if he had stepped out of a hot bath and been startled by the coldness of the air.

'No, this is my first,' replied the small woman with the soft speckled eyes and the gentle look of a domesticated cat.

There were six passengers at the dining table that evening for their first meal together: the small woman, the red-faced man and his sullen thin-faced wife, two young men and a middle-aged woman, her blonde hair scraped back into a tight bun.

'We've been on over twenty,' boasted the red-faced man, thrusting out his jaw. 'Haven't we Beryl?'

'If you say so,' his wife replied. She closed her eyes and puckered her lips.

'We've been up the Baltic, down the fjords, through the Panama Canal, around the Canaries, and across the Atlantic. Last year we was on the "Cradles of Civilisation" cruise in the Med., wasn't we Beryl?'

'Yes, we was,' muttered his wife.

'That must have been very interesting,' said the small woman.

'Not really,' the man replied, shaking his head. 'Not my cup of tea all these old ruins. I mean once you've seen one, you've seen them all, haven't you? Anyway we always do the Christmas cruise to get away from all the bad weather and to escape from the carryings-on back home, don't we Beryl?'

'Yes,' his wife replied morosely, looking into the middle distance.

'I'm so much looking forward to the cruise,' the small woman told those at the table. 'I can't remember when I was so excited.'

One of the young men was about to reply but the red-faced man was quick to answer, 'Yes, well if you want to know anything, you know where to come.'

'It's a lovely boat,' she said.

'Ship, love. It's a ship,' he told her with a self-satisfied look on his round face.

The small lady smiled.

The red-faced man turned his attention to the two young men. 'First time for you too as well, is it?' he asked.

'Pardon?'

'First cruise you've been on?'

'Yes, it is,' one young man replied.

'And what about you?' the red-faced man asked the woman with the blonde hair.

'No,' she replied curtly. 'I've cruised before.'

'Many times?' he asked, thrusting out his jaw again.

'This will be my fortieth.'

'Bloody Nora!' exclaimed the red-faced man. 'You're hardly off of the ship.'

'I'm the port lecturer,' she told him, smiling stiffly. 'I do spend a great deal of my time cruising.'

'Port lecturer,' he repeated. 'Well, I hope you're more interesting than the last chap we had. Some dusty old professor. Looked as if he'd been dug up and his talks were as dry as ditch water. He could put a glass eye to sleep.' He laughed at his own witticism.

'Hey, do you remember Beryl, when we went in to hear him just after lunch and he turned the lights off to show some slides and most of the people fell asleep. When the lights came on again this bloke on the front row was snoring like I don't know what. "Is this man with you, madam?" he asked the woman sitting next to the snoring chap and she said she was his wife. "Well will you wake him up," said the lecturer. "You put him to sleep," she replied. "You wake him up."' He roared with laughter. His wife raised an eyebrow and sighed. No doubt she had heard this many times before.

'Well, I shall endeavour to be a little more fascinating for you,' remarked the port lecturer slowly and with great emphasis, leaning forward slightly in her chair.

The sarcasm was not lost on the red-faced man. He gave a dismissive grunt, lowered his face and examined the menu.

They ordered their meals.

'So, what do you do for a living?' the red-faced man asked the two young men after a while.

'We're solicitors,' one replied.

'I own a factory,' he told them, leaning back expansively on his chair. 'Recycling waste products. You'd be amazed how much stuff people chuck out. Employ twenty men I do. I left school with not one susstificate and never had no need to have all these qualifications and prefixes after my name. And I'll tell you what, I've made a bob or two in the process.' He held up a wrist to display his showy gold watch. 'Rolex. State of the Ark engineering is that.'

He turned his attention back to the small woman. 'So, what's your cabin like then?'

'Very nice,' she replied.

'We've an outside cabin with a double balcony and fully equipped bathroom. Much larger than most and with a bath, haven't we Beryl?'

His wife sighed. 'Yes, we have.'

'We're on Deck A at the front. I can't be doing with an inside cabin. I get claustropthermia. I have to have a window and I like to be at the front of the ship.'

'Forwards,' said one of the young men.

'Beg pardon?'

'I think the front of a ship is referred to as the forward.'

The red-faced man gave a grunt and cast the speaker

a look of barely suppressed animosity. 'We're right next to the captain's state room,' he said. 'We've sailed with Captain Pierpont a few times before. Very good captain. Youngest in the fleet and not stand-offish like some I could mention. I expect we'll be asked to his Christmas cocktail party tomorrow night.' He looked pointedly at the young man who had put him right. 'Course, not all the passengers are invited.'

The red-faced man was quiet for a few minutes as he ate his meal but soon interrupted the port lecturer who was explaining to the two young men how to book the various excursions.

'I suppose you get them free,' he remarked, dabbing his fat lips with a napkin.

'Do I get what free?' she asked. Her gaze was expressionless.

'The trips,' he said.

'I'm the port lecturer. It is part of my job to accompany the passengers.' She turned to the two young men and then smiled at the small woman and raised an eyebrow. 'I hope I will see you on the excursions. They are most interesting and informative and we have local guides to point out areas of interest. When we dock—'

'We don't bother with the excursions, do we Beryl?' remarked the red-faced man. 'We make our own way. It's cheaper for a start and you're not herded along like cattle. I think you see more of the country if you go around yourself.'

The port lecturer's mouth tightened and an angry spot showed itself on each of her cheeks. It was with some difficulty that she controlled herself. 'Really,' she said. 'Then I suggest you do that.' She turned to the others at the table. 'If you will excuse me,' she said, rising to her feet, 'I have a lecture to prepare for tomorrow.'

'And we will say good evening as well,' added one of the young men and they both departed.

'So how much did you pay for the cruise?', the red-faced man asked the small woman.

'I didn't pay anything,' the small woman told him smiling. 'My son booked it for me. He said "you can't be on your own at Christmas, mother". I lost my husband ten years' ago. Robert, he's my son, said I needed to have people around me at this time of year, not stuck at home on my own. He's a good lad is Robert. He travels a lot you see otherwise we would have had Christmas together at home.'

'He probably got some special deal for you,' observed the red-faced man.

'Probably,' agreed the woman. 'Well, I think I'll make my excuses and go and hear the concert pianist.'

'Oh, we won't be bothering with all that plinky-plonky music,' said the red-faced man, 'and we shan't be going to the show either. Last year the comedian was about as funny as haemorrhoids and as for the singer –'

'Why don't you shut up complaining!' interrupted his wife sharply, 'and drink your coffee!'

The red-faced man and his long-suffering wife did not appear for dinner the following evening much to the relief of the other passengers at the table who enjoyed a most good-humoured conversation. It was the following morning when the small woman met the red-faced man and his wife drinking coffee in the Crow's Nest Bar.

'Good morning,' she said brightly.

'Oh, hello,' said the man. His wife nodded.

'We missed you at the dinner table last night. Were you not feeling well?'

'We decided to have dinner on our own,' the man replied. 'Nothing personal and present company excepted but we didn't take to the others on the table.'

'*You* didn't,' said his wife pointedly, thinking she

was now destined to spend two weeks listening to his overbearing dogmatic tones.

'I found that port lecturer woman far too hoity-toity for my liking,' the red-faced man continued. 'She's only an employee and it was as if she owned the ship. I shall have a word with the purser about her. And as for the two lawyers, well they had no conversation at all, sat there like stuffed dummies.'

'Unlike you,' murmured his wife.

'On the last cruise we had a right lively time, didn't we Beryl?'

'Not really,' she replied. 'I was glad to get home.'

'We did,' he said. 'We had a right old laugh with what's-his-name who owned the pet shop.'

'Cyril.'

'Aye, Cyril. He could have been on stage and much better than the comedian they had on the ship.'

'He was a pain in the neck,' said his wife, 'and he was vulgar too.'

The red-faced man changed the subject. 'I reckon them two chaps on the table are gay you know.'

'Really,' said the small woman before adding, 'and that bothers you, does it?'

'No, I've nothing against that sort of people, it's just that I don't have to spend a fortnight at the same table.'

'I'm pleased you have nothing against gay people,' said the small woman. 'I really find those who are prejudiced extremely sad and ignorant and very unpleasant people, don't you think?'

'Yes, well,' said the man, his face assuming an ever darker shade of red. For a rare moment he was lost for words.

'Well, there's the port lecturer,' the small woman informed him. 'She's about to start her lecture so I will be on my way.'

'We'll not be joining you,' said the red-faced man.

'I will,' said his wife, rising from her chair.

At that moment the captain, resplendent in his white uniform with gold stripes on his sleeves, appeared and began chatting with the passengers.

The red-faced man sat up. 'Oh, there's Captain Pierpont,' he said. 'He often walks round the ship in the mornings to talk to people.' The captain looked in his direction, smiled and waved a hand. The red-faced man felt a glow of satisfaction as he saw the captain heading his way. 'It's the Christmas cocktail party this evening,' he said. 'I guess he'll be inviting certain passengers – the seasoned cruisers.' He turned to the small woman. 'Well, I'll not keep you,' he told her dismissively. 'I'll let you get off to your lecture.'

'Good morning,' said the captain, approaching the three passengers.

'Good morning captain,' said the red-faced man, standing and holding out a fat hand.

The captain bent and kissed the small woman warmly on the cheek.

'Now remember,' he said, 'cocktails at seven-thirty and dinner at eight and wear your best frock. You're on the captain's table this evening. And you might like to bring your dining companions with you.'

'I will,' the small woman replied. She looked at the red-faced man who was standing mouth open like a fish on a marble slab. 'This is my son, Robert,' she said. 'I'm sorry, I didn't catch *your* name.'

THE CHRISTMAS POET

A PLAY

May I help you?

Yes, I'm the poet.

Who?

The visiting poet, invited into school to read some Christmas poems to the children.

I don't think you're expected.

I was invited.

Nobody's told me. Mind you, nobody tells me anything.

I'm just the school secretary.

Miss Drinkwater arranged it.

She's left.

Oh.

She went off with stress after the school inspection.

I see.

Had a bit of a breakdown.

Oh dear.

Took early retirement.

Well, I have travelled quite a distance to be here today.

Wait here. I'll get the head teacher.

May I help you? I'm Miss Bracegirdle, the head teacher.

Good morning. I'm the poet.

The poet?

*The visiting poet, invited into school to read some Christmas
poems to the children.*

You're not expected.

Miss Drinkwater arranged it.

She's left.

So I believe.

She went off with stress after the school inspection.

She didn't cancel my visit.

Well I think that poetry was the last thing on her mind
after what the inspectors said about her and the state she
got in. Anyway, now that you are here, I suppose you had
better stay. If you would like to wait in the staffroom.

I have a parent in to see me. Ah, here comes Mr Snoddy, the caretaker. He'll show you where it is. Mr Snoddy, would you show this gentleman to the staffroom please? *Good morning.*

Are you here about the toilets?

No, I'm the poet.

Who?

The visiting poet, invited into school to read some Christmas poems to the children.

I didn't know there was a poet in school this morning. Mind you nobody tells me anything. I'm just the school caretaker.

Miss Drinkwater arranged it.

She's left.

So I believe.

Came down with stress after the school inspection. Locked herself in the ladies for two hours before we could get her out. You don't know anything about toilets by any chance, do you?

No, I'm afraid not.

Well, here's the staffroom. I'll leave you with Mrs Marshbank. I need to see to the toilets.

Good morning.

Morning. Don't set your books up on that table. We have our coffee on there.

Who do you imagine I am?

You're the book rep aren't you?

No, I'm the poet.

Who?

The visiting poet, invited into school to read some Christmas poems to the children.

I didn't know you were coming in. You're not on the notice board. Mind you nobody tells me anything around here. I'm just the classroom assistant.

Miss Drinkwater arranged it.

She's left.

Took early retirement, I believe.

Yes.

After the inspection.

Did you know Miss Drinkwater?

No, I never met her.

And you're a poet?

Yes.

I can't say that I'm very keen on poetry myself.

Really?

I mean, it's not as if poetry is going to get anybody a job?

Unless they become a poet.

Pardon?

It doesn't matter.

Don't get me wrong. I do like some poetry – funny poems that rhyme.

I see.

Are your poems funny?

Some are.

Do they rhyme?

Some do.

Well I must get on. I've got the slow reading group next. Still here, Mrs Marshbank?

I'm just going Miss Windthropp.

Now then Mr—?

Crispin.

We have a bit of a problem.

Oh.

The vicar is in school this morning to take the Christmas assembly. He does tend to ramble on so what I thought is perhaps you could do half an hour after the Reverend Plackett has finished.

Half an hour?

The children won't be able to sit still for much longer.

We have our fair share of fidgeters and several pupils with attention deficit.

I was booked to spend the full day here.

That's not possible I'm afraid. We've got the school nurse in later this morning checking for head lice, then the rehearsal for the Nativity Play and later this afternoon the interviews for Miss Drinkwater's replacement. I think I told you she's left. Half an hour will be quite sufficient. By the way, you have been vetted haven't you?

Vetted?

Vetted by the police.

No.

Everyone coming into contact with children these days has to be checked by the police to make sure they haven't got a criminal record.

I haven't got a criminal record.

That's as may be, but you have to be checked. Have you got a CRB?

A CRB?

A certificate from the Criminal Records Bureau.

No.

What about a clearance from the DBS?

DBS?

Disclosure and Barring Service.

No, I've not. I've never heard of them.

Then I'm afraid I can't let you near the children.

Miss Drinkwater never mentioned anything about being vetted by the CRB or the DBS.

She had a lot on her mind, as I think I explained.

So I can't read my poems to the children?

I'm afraid not. We have to be very careful these days.

Well, I may as well go then.

If you get vetted, Mr Crispin, get in touch and I am sure we can set something up, maybe for Christmas and you could double as our Father Christmas.

12

HAPPY CHRISTMAS, MISS DUNN

A SHORT STORY

Kyle arrived at Miss Dunn's classroom three weeks before the end of the school term. He was small for his ten years with a mane of dusty blond hair tied back in a ponytail, a brown, healthy-looking face and eyes as grey as the winter sky outside. He was dressed in a bizarre mixture of clothes: baggy red shirt, denim jacket embroidered with birds and animals, plum coloured corduroy trousers and sturdy green leather boots.

'Ah, Miss Dunn,' the young head teacher said with his usual forced joviality and silly smile. 'There you are.'

Where else would I be, thought the teacher looking up

from her desk without replying. Each morning, regular as the ticking clock on the wall, she would be in her classroom marking the children's work and preparing for the day ahead. She had done this every day for all the thirty five years she had been in the teaching profession. She wasn't likely to change the habit of a lifetime.

The young head teacher, still holding the smile, directed the boy through the door with a gentle push.

'We have a new addition to our school,' he told Miss Dunn, patting the child on the shoulder. 'This is Kyle and he will be joining your class for the time being.'

The teacher smiled at the strange little individual who stood before her and stared around the room with wide inquisitive eyes. For a child to start a new school and not look in the least nervous surprised Miss Dunn.

'Hello, Kyle,' she said pleasantly.

'Say hello to your new teacher, Kyle,' prompted the young head teacher before the boy could respond.

'Hello,' said the child cheerfully.

'And you must call your teacher "miss", when you speak to her,' said the new head teacher.

'Hello, miss,' said the boy. 'How are you?' He held out his hand.

'I am very well thank you,' replied Miss Dunn, shaking his small hand, 'and how are you?'

'Well, I'm not too bad,' he replied with what might be interpreted as a cheeky smile. Miss Dunn wondered if he was being deliberately impertinent.

'Well, it's nice to see you Kyle,' said the teacher, 'and I hope you'll settle in and—'

'I'll have a word with you at morning break, Miss Dunn,' the new young head teacher interrupted. He gave her a knowing look – a look which said there were things about this child that she needed to know. 'I am now going to take young Kyle to my room, Miss Dunn, and explain to him how we do things here at St Mary's, how we all behave ourselves, follow the rules, work hard, do our very best and how we all pull together and get along as one big happy family.' Miss Dunn raised an eyebrow in wordless contradiction. If the man thought this school was 'one big happy family' he was a bigger fool than she thought. 'We also have a school uniform policy here, Kyle,' continued the young head teacher cheerfully and maintaining his inane expression, 'so—'

'My father's not into uniforms,' interrupted the boy. 'He thinks they stop people being individuals.'

The young head teacher coloured and the bright artificial smile disappeared. A sudden irritation darkened his face. Miss Dunn quite enjoyed his discomfiture and tried to suppress a smile. 'Well, perhaps I need to have a word with your father,' he said, with an edge to his voice. Then, turning to Miss Dunn, he spoke in a noticeably less than cheerful voice, 'I'll bring him back at the start of the lesson and, as I said, would appreciate a word with you at morning break.'

'I'm on yard duty,' she informed him.

'I'll arrange for Mrs Wellbeloved to cover for you,' he said sharply.

That would go down like a bad case of the flu, thought Miss Dunn. She could visualise her colleague's face when she was told she would have to give up her morning break and brave the cold snowy weather outside.

Miss Dunn did not return to her marking. She stared at the scene through the classroom window. The snow had fallen softly overnight and the whole area around the small school was a vast white silent sea. She sighed. *Another child to add to an already unwieldy class*, she thought despondently, *and probably a little handful as well by the looks of him.*

Miss Dunn had taught difficult and deprived children on leaving college: grubby little scraps from homes where there was precious little self-esteem and expectation – two things she always regarded as important if a child was to succeed in life. And of course there were no books. Theirs was a background of deprivation, unemployment, family difficulties, absentee fathers, limited aspirations, few opportunities for the children to better themselves and very often verbal and sometimes physical abuse. She could tell by their unhealthy sallow complexions that their staple diet would be largely chips and crisps and fast food and that many of them would be up half the night watching the most unsuitable of television programmes. She had seen it so many times before. Those children hadn't much of a chance in life. They were difficult and demanding at the start but once they got to know her and knew that she wanted the best for them they began to behave. They were grateful to have someone who took an interest in them, had time to listen and show them some affection. They had cried when she had told them she was leaving and had bought her a present of a cheap china figurine of a woman in a pale blue crinoline dress and holding a parasol. She had it on her sideboard at home.

The children who attended St Mary's were very different. On the whole they were quiet, biddable and well-behaved but there was precious little gratitude from them or their parents and even the most exciting of topics she taught seemed to hold little interest for them. Her pupils came from affluent homes with parents who had high aspirations for them – sometimes unrealistically high. They were over-indulged children living in their large detached houses with their own bedrooms, computers and televisions, holidaying abroad and with every new gadget, game and toy money could buy.

The new boy intrigued her with his clear grey eyes and ready smile. As she thought about him she wondered what home he came from. He certainly wasn't a dirty or a neglected child. Indeed the small cold hand which she shook and the long blond hair were as clean as any child's in her class. But who would send a child to school like that? Dressed in his red shirt and coloured jacket and pants he would look out of place amongst the grey school uniforms of the St Mary's children, a strange exotic bird caught in a flock of sparrows.

Miss Dunn could tell, of course, by the expression on the young head teacher's face that the boy would probably spell trouble. No doubt the child's record from his previous school – if indeed he had attended a previous school – had been scrutinised and the catalogue of his misbehaviour duly noted. She knew that the most confident and well-adjusted child often finds it difficult starting a new school, particularly when it was well into the term. It was never easy for the new pupil to settle in, make friends, and get used to the routines and the rules, the unfamiliar environment and the strange faces. For a child like this one – so very different from his peers – it would prove even more difficult. And yet, he seemed in no way disconcerted or nervous when she met him. *The child would undoubtedly have special needs*, thought the teacher. There was no question about that. His reading would be well below standard, his writing weak and his number work poor. She thought of the disproportionate amount of time she would have to spend to get him up to an acceptable standard and she would get precious little support from home or indeed from the young head teacher. And yet there was something about the child which made her think that she may be misjudging him and that she might enjoy the challenge. He might very well liven things up in the class. And was he really trying to be impudent when he smiled at her, when he looked her straight in the eye and held out his hand or was he genuinely being friendly?

The snow had turned to sleet outside and icy droplets trickled down the windows. She smiled at the thought of Mrs Wellbeloved and her reaction when she was told she would be on yard duty that morning break. She visualised the angry downturn of the mouth and the complaining voice increasing in pitch and agitation.

Miss Dunn shook her head and looked down at the exercise book before her on the desk. The child's poem, entitled 'Winter' which she was marking, like all the rest she had read through that morning, was neat enough, the spellings were good and the punctuation sound but it was tiresome in its banality.

The snow is like a big white blanket that covers
    all the ground.
There are no leaves on the trees and no birds
    around.
I like it in winter when the cold wind does blow
And you can go outside and play in all the snow.

What had been the point, she thought, of spending all of Sunday evening preparing a lesson which had clearly had little effect? What had been the point of trying to inspire children with the same sense of awe and wonder as she felt whenever she looked out on a winter scene? Better perhaps to have done what Mrs Wellbeloved usually did with her class: give the children a worksheet. 'I don't know why you bother,' her colleague had told her in the staffroom one lunchtime. 'I am a big believer in work-sheets. They save on the marking and all that wretched preparation. They occupy the children, keep them quiet and the parents like it when they see their children's books full up with plenty of writing.'

Miss Dunn knew there was more to teaching than that. She had talked to the children about her childhood and how she loved the wintertime. She had told them how when she was their age she would jump out of bed in the morning, the lino cold on her bare feet and she would scratch the ice from the window pane with her nails to peer through. She had been so excited when she saw the great flakes of snow falling like goose down, settling and gradually forming a thick carpet along the pavements outside. Walls, trees, road signs, letter boxes, rooftops were soon shrouded in white. Then the snow would begin in earnest and an icy wind would rage. School would be cancelled and all day she would play out with her brother, competing who could build the biggest and best snowman. Cold and wet and tired they would then abandon their creations and return to the house for hot soup and sit before the fire. Sometimes when the snow began to melt they would get wrapped up and their father would pack them in the car with its noisy engine and leather seats and take them to the coast at Whitby. They would brave the cold wind, hair stiff with salt, and walk the cliff top path, looking down at the gun-metal grey ocean beneath them, the forests of white crests, the oily waves circling and arching and the seaweed glittering wet. There was not one other person to be seen. It was like another world. She had gathered the class around her and read her favourite winter poem, talked about the vivid imagery and the vocabulary and how Shakespeare created the atmosphere of winter:

When icicles hang by the wall,
And Dick the shepherd blows his nail,
And Tom bears logs into the hall,

And milk comes frozen home in pail,
When blood is nipp'd and ways be foul,
Then nightly sings the staring owl,
Tu-whit;
Tu-who, a merry note,
While greasy Joan doth keel the pot.

The children had settled down to write their own poems
and all she got was:

The snow is like a big white blanket that covers
all the ground.
There are no leaves on the trees and no birds
around.

Perhaps, thought Miss Dunn, it was time for her to go,
to leave teaching. She was nearing sixty and could retire
comfortably with her pension and with her severance
pay. She could join a night class, spend more time in the
garden, take up golf, devote more energy to the charities
she supported. Mrs Wellbeloved, the teacher of the
eleven-year-olds, who sat in the corner of the staffroom,
clacking away with her knitting needles like Madame

Defarge, the fictional character in the novel by Charles Dickens who knitted in the shadow of the guillotine, spent most of her time regaling anyone willing enough to listen, how she was counting the days to her retirement. 'I'll be glad to get out,' was her recurrent announcement. 'If I had my time over again (click-clack), I should never go in for teaching (click-clack). I've put my own children off, I can tell you that (click-clack). Standards have plummeted (click-clack), children are so badly behaved these days (click-clack), parents are a pain in the neck (click-clack) and then there's all this bloody paperwork (click-clack).'

Miss Dunn had to admit that her colleague had a point on some things. It was tough going these days. Children in her class were not misbehaved but their parents had become increasingly demanding and interfering and the Government had buried the teachers in a snowstorm of paperwork. There were guidelines and directives, policy documents and curriculum statements coming over the hills like the Plagues of Egypt. Then there was the young head teacher with all his initiatives and brainwaves. Teaching was indeed very different now from when she had started.

Miss Dunn had always considered herself to be a good teacher. She prepared her lessons meticulously, marked the books rigorously, mounted colourful displays and, until the new head teacher had put a stop to it because of the potential risks, taken children out of school on outings to the castle, the canal and the museum. She tried to make her lessons interesting and participatory. She produced the Nativity Play each year and coached the school choir. She knew she would never win the 'Teacher of the Year' Award but she was dedicated and hard-working and gave the children the best she could give. But her best did not seem good enough for the new head teacher. When he arrived bubbling with enthusiasm he brought with him a band-wagon crammed full of every educational initiative and strategy that was doing the rounds and a new language full of jargon, psychobabble and gobbledegook. She had to smile. She could see the head teacher describing the new addition to the school on the computerised record system he had recently introduced. 'Kyle is a behaviourally challenged student from a multi-delin-quent family with siblings high on the incarceration index.'

Soon after his arrival the new head teacher had observed some of her lessons in a bid to 'get to know my staff.' At her first appraisal meeting after the observations he informed her that ('please don't take this the wrong way, Miss Dunn, I am merely trying to be constructive') that he felt her lessons 'lacked a certain rigour' and that she 'did not sparkle.' She told the young head teacher that she was not some sort of fairy which lit up on the top of a Christmas tree, she was a teacher with an unblemished record and over thirty years' experience in the classroom. Of course, she had been upset. He had smiled in that patronising way of his and he told her that he wanted all those 'on the St Mary's Team' to 'come aboard', 'think outside the box' and 'get up to speed.' She had told him that, at her time of life, it was difficult 'for a leopard to change its spots', to 'put old wine into new bottles' and for 'an old dog to learn new tricks.' He informed her that they did not seem to be speaking the same language. It was the first occasion that she had agreed with him.

The bell rang shrilly and her reverie ended abruptly. A moment later the children entered the classroom, as they always did, in a quiet and orderly manner. They never burst through the door chattering excitedly like most children of their age would, they never challenged the teacher and seldom volunteered opinions despite her efforts to get them to contribute in the lessons. They sat there in their smart pristine uniforms and with serious faces, like empty vessels waiting to be filled up with facts. It was they who 'did not sparkle,' she thought.

Kyle arrived by himself a moment later. He sauntered in with his hands behind his back. All eyes turned in his direction. There were whispers and smirks and a few giggles but he seemed oblivious and walked to the front of the room. Miss Dunn stared at her class and her brow furrowed. All noise ceased.

'That's right, come along in Kyle,' she said cheerfully to the boy. 'You can sit here at the front.' *Best to keep an eye on him*, she thought.

'Thank you,' he said, walking towards her in a slow and relaxed manner with what she thought might be something of a swagger.

He sat down at the desk, stretched his legs, rested his hands on the top and looked around him with a curious expression on his face.

Miss Dunn was intrigued. In her experience children new to a school usually hovered indecisively in the doorway of the classroom. They were nervous and shy. This boy was supremely confident.

'Now children, sit up and look this way please,' instructed the teacher. 'This is Kyle and he will be joining our class. I want you all to make him feel at home and help him to settle in.' She knew this was an idle request and that none of the children would have anything to do with him. 'It must be rather daunting for someone to join a new school so I expect you all to be friendly and helpful.' The boy did not look at all daunted, she thought, catching sight of his smiling face. Then she added, the tone of her voice changing, 'And should I hear of anyone being unkind or unpleasant in any way, then they will have me to answer to.'

When the children had settled down to their silent reading, Miss Dunn sat next to the new boy and explained what they had been doing in the previous lesson. She noticed the fierce look of concentration on the child's face as he listened to her and the brightness of his large round eyes. There was a faint but not unpleasant smell about him of spices and wood smoke.

'The children have written a poem about winter,' she explained softly, bending closer towards him. 'Here's a copy of the poem I read to the class. Don't worry if you find it a little difficult. It is a very old poem and some of the words you might not understand. Just try your best.'

The boy studied the paper. 'There's another verse to this,' he said.

Miss Dunn was startled. 'Yes, indeed there is.'

'It's by Shakespeare, isn't it?'

'It is indeed.'

'It's one of my favourites. My father says it captures the essence of winter.' Then the boy recited.

When all aloud the wind doth blow,
And coughing drowns the parson's saw,
And birds sit brooding in the snow,
And Marion's nose looks red and raw,
When roasted crabs hiss in the bowl,
Then nightly sings the staring owl,
Tu-whit;
Tu-who, a merry note,
While greasy Joan doth keel the pot.

'Good gracious, Kyle!' exclaimed Miss Dunn. 'You know it by heart.'

'I like to learn poems,' the boy told her, leaning back in his chair. 'My father's a poet and a musician as well as a woodcarver. We don't have a television so we spend most evenings in the van reading and talking and making things. Sometimes we write and learn poems. My father says that the best way of saying something is through a poem. It has a special sort of language.'

Miss Dunn was momentarily lost for words. 'Well,' she said at last, 'perhaps you would like to write a poem this morning.'

'Yes, I should like that,' replied the boy.

'So you see,' explained the new head teacher to Miss Dunn at morning break, 'the boy lives in a caravan with his father who appears to be something of an itinerant. Never stays in one place for long, from what I can gather. He's one of these so-called New Age travellers. The boy seems to have spent very little time in school. Hopefully, he won't be with us after Christmas.'

'Why do you say "hopefully"?,' enquired Miss Dunn.

'Well, let's be honest, he's hardly likely to settle in here is he?' asked the new head teacher. 'I mean you've seen the state in which he's come to school and you heard what his father thinks about uniform. I have to say that when I met his father when he brought the boy in this morning, I guessed we would encounter problems. He was a very odd looking individual. Anyway I found out from him the name of the last school the boy attended and contacted the head teacher who confirmed my opinion. He said the boy was a very strange and rather outspoken child who didn't mix with the other children. Far too much to say for himself according to his last teacher who was relieved that he has moved on. I have an idea the boy will be a handful.'

'The boy does have a name,' Miss Dunn told him. 'It's Kyle.'

'I am aware what he is called,' he retorted sharply.

'And he seems very pleasant.'

The new head teacher gave a dismissive grunt. 'That's as may be but give it time. Once he's settled in he will show his true colours.'

'I thought you said he would be unlikely to settle in here,' remarked Miss Dunn.

'I suggest you keep a sharp eye on the boy,' said the head teacher, deciding to ignore the pointed comment. 'And should you experience any trouble with him, he should to be sent to me.'

Miss Dunn caught sight of Mrs Wellbeloved through the window, stomping through the slush in the playground with a disgruntled look on her face. She allowed herself a small smile. She considered relieving her of yard duty but thought better of it and decided to make herself a cup of coffee in the staffroom.

'That will be all thank you, Miss Dunn,' said the head teacher dismissively.

Miss Dunn was taken aback again during the lunch hour when she examined Kyle's work. She had watched him earlier that morning writing slowly and with deliberation, his tongue sticking out from the corner of his mouth. He occasionally gazed out of the classroom window, as if deep in thought, at other times he stared at the floor and closed his eyes as if in prayer. When the bell rang for morning break, he had presented her with a neatly-written and vivid poem on winter where 'icicles hung from the guttering like Winter's fangs' and 'snow crusted in billows', where 'black skeletal trees clawed a cold and empty sky' and 'rooks like scraps of black cloth were tossed in the fierce wind.' *He couldn't have written this*, thought Miss Dunn. No child of ten could possibly have composed a piece of verse of such originality, descriptive beauty and sophistication. But she soon discovered that he had and for the remainder of the week he continued to produce work of such startling quality that Miss Dunn was left spellbound. The child had a great capacity for astonishing her, never less than his vocabulary. She had never in her career come across a young writer so talented.

'You have a rare gift, Kyle,' she told the boy one lunchtime. She found him in the school library poring over a book. 'I have never come across anyone of your age who can write with such flair and inventiveness.'

'Thank you,' he said, his smile broadening. 'I do enjoy words. I think I would like to be an author when I grow up.'

'Well, I look forward to hearing great things about you in the future and reading your novels and poetry. And how are you settling in?'

The boy thought for a moment and a small smile came to his lips. 'I don't really settle into any school,' he replied. 'I've been to so many and I think it best not to try and make friends and get used to things. Actually I like my own company. My father doesn't like to stay too long in any one place. He's a free spirit you see. He likes to be out on the road and in the fresh air.'

'So you'll be moving on then?' asked the teacher.

'I guess so,' replied the boy. 'One of these fine days.'

'And how is the new boy getting along?' the new head teacher asked Miss Dunn the following week. It was morning break and he was pinning yet another Government directive on the notice board in the staff-room.

'Very well,' the teacher replied simply. She kept her exchanges with the new head teacher as brief as possible.

'He needs a good wash from what I've seen of him,' Mrs Wellbeloved observed from the corner of the staff-room, producing her knitting needles from a capacious canvas bag. She wrinkled her nose slightly as if there were

a faintly unpleasant odour in the room. 'And whatever is he wearing? He's like a walking jumble sale. I wasn't aware the school rule on uniform had been relaxed.'

'The school uniform policy has most certainly not been relaxed,' the head teacher told her, clearly stung by his colleague's comment. 'I have written to the boy's father on two occasions and received no reply.'

'As regards needing a wash,' said Miss Dunn, 'Kyle is a very clean boy and what is more, he is highly intelligent and very well-behaved.'

'I would never have guessed it from the look of him,' said Mrs Wellbeloved, starting to clack away with her needles. She was knitting a garish black and yellow jumper. Miss Dunn smiled to think of her colleague wearing such an item. With her large menacing bust and huge hips, she would look like a giant wasp buzzing about the school. She was the very last person who should comment unfavourably on other people's dress, enthroned as she was in the corner chair wearing a shapeless lavender hand-knitted cashmere twin set.

'Looks can be deceptive,' she said.

'Well, someone should have a word about the uniform (click-clack),' said Mrs Wellbeloved. She gave a wintry smile. 'It lets the school down having a child coming here dressed like that. He stands out like the proverbial sore thumb.'

'His father's not into uniform,' remarked Miss Dunn. It was a carefully and cleverly aimed provocation.

'Well, I am!' snapped the head teacher. 'I predicted from the start the boy would be something of a problem.'

'He isn't a problem,' said Miss Dunn. 'Quite the reverse.'

'Of course they never stay long these gypsy types (click-clack),' said her colleague, ignoring the comment. 'They are a damn nuisance when they are here (click-clack) and you should see the mess they leave behind when they decide to leave.'

'He's a nice little boy,' said Miss Dunn airily.

'He looks bizarre (click-clack),' said Mrs Wellbeloved. 'A very odd child in those strange clothes and ridiculous boots and his hair wants cutting. He looks like a girl.'

'He doesn't seem to mix,' said the head teacher, testily. 'I have been monitoring him from my window at break times and he tends to sit on the wall by himself with a book or wander around the playground or spend time in the library. He should make more of an effort to mix with the other children. I think I might ask the educational psychologist to have a word with him.'

'Perhaps you ought to leave him alone,' said Miss Dunn sharply. 'There are people in the world, me included, who do like to read and are quite happy in their own company.'

'I bet he's bullied, the way he dresses (click-clack),' observed Mrs Wellbeloved.

'Well, he isn't,' Miss Dunn told her.

'One can't be too sure,' remarked the head teacher.

'I am,' said Miss Dunn.

'What's his background (click-clack)?' asked Mrs Wellbeloved. She sniffed self-righteously. 'He looks like a little gypsy to me.'

'We don't say "gypsy" any more, Mrs Wellbeloved,' the head teacher told her. 'The term we use now is "traveller". His father is one of these so-called "new-age travellers".'

The teacher made a loud clucking noise with her tongue. 'Another example of political correctness,' she remarked. 'Well, I would watch your purse, Joyce, if I were you (click-clack).'

'And I should be grateful, Miss Dunn,' said the head teacher, 'if you would have a word with the boy about the uniform and not to wear those boots. We cannot have him coming to school dressed as he is. I think you also need to mention his hair. It needs cutting. I am always rather distrustful of men with long hair.'

'I thought St Mary's was a church school?' asked Miss Dunn.

'It is a church school,' retorted the head teacher.

'Well long hair was good enough for Jesus,' she remarked, 'and I think of all people, He could be trusted.'

The Saturday before the school broke up for the Christmas holidays, Miss Dunn was making her way through the crowds in the arcade in the centre of the town. She had few presents to buy and had posted all her cards but she enjoyed the busy, colourful atmosphere in the shops at Christmastime so decided not to go home. In the very centre of the arcade was a large Nativity scene containing huge garish plaster figures of the Holy Family, the shepherds and the Magi surrounded by a variety of toy animals. Tinny piped music was playing. Miss Dunn thought how tasteless it looked and how very different it was from the stable in which the Baby Jesus was born. Then she spotted Kyle. He was standing by the escalator, a cap full of small change before him, playing a tin whistle. His eyes were set firmly on the man accompanying him on an old fiddle. He was a tall striking-looking individual with long blond hair tied back in a ponytail, dressed in bright but shabby clothes. A heavy boot tapped the floor and kept time with the music. Miss Dunn watched fascinated. She waited until they stopped and started to gather up the change and then approached.

'Hello Kyle,' she said. 'I didn't know you were a musician as well.'

If the boy was embarrassed, he didn't show it. 'Hello, Miss Dunn,' he said pleasantly. The tall man with him swivelled around. 'This is my teacher, father.'

'How do you do,' said the man, staring with penetrating grey eyes.

'My father plays the fiddle,' said Kyle. 'He's a street entertainer.'

'So I see,' replied the teacher.

'I hope my son is behaving himself in your class,' said the boy's father.

'He's a pleasure to teach,' Miss Dunn told him.

'I'm pleased to hear it,' said the man, putting a hand on the boy's shoulder. 'He's a good lad.'

'I'm glad I've met you,' said Miss Dunn as the man started to put his violin in a battered case. 'I have been wanting to have a word with you about Kyle.'

'Ah, the uniform,' sighed the man, smiling.

'No, not the uniform. I would like to talk to you about Kyle's work. Perhaps you could call into school sometime next week?'

'I am afraid I don't really like schools,' said the boy's father. 'I never have and I never will. They teach children things which are not worth knowing. They try and change them. The only reason Kyle is at school at the moment is to get the truant officer off my back and save me a court appearance.'

'Nevertheless—' began Miss Dunn.

'Look, Miss—'

'Dunn.'

'Look, Miss Dunn,' said the man moving closer to her. 'Kyle and me get on just fine without school. We don't want people trying to change us, to make us conform, to be something we don't wish to be.'

'I'm not trying to change Kyle,' said the teacher. 'I wouldn't want him to change. He's like a breath of fresh air in my classroom. He's a very gifted young writer. In all my years as a teacher, I have never come across work of such quality from a ten-year-old child. He has a lively, enquiring mind and his poems—'

The man held up a hand. 'I know Miss Dunn,' he said. 'I know that Kyle has a real talent and I don't want that talent stifled. I want it to flourish and that is why I don't want him in school.'

'I like Miss Dunn, father,' said Kyle who had been listening to the exchange. 'She's the best teacher I have ever had. She listens and helps and doesn't try to change me.'

'Well, I am grateful for that,' said the boy's father, 'and I thank her for all the time and effort but we shall be moving on tomorrow.' He put his arm around his son's shoulder. 'We like to travel, you see. We like to be outdoors, free spirits, Kyle and me. We can't be tied down to anywhere or anybody. Can you understand that, Miss Dunn?'

'Yes, I think I can,' said the teacher. She looked at the

boy and then held out her hand. 'Goodbye Kyle. I shall miss you.'

As she walked away, for some strange reason, tears began to prick her eyes.

'Miss Dunn!' The boy ran after her. He pressed a small, beautifully-carved pale wood figure of the Virgin and Child into her hand. 'My father did it,' he told her. 'It's for you. Happy Christmas, Miss Dunn.'

13

A CHRISTMAS MIRACLE

A SHORT STORY

The lonely farmhouse stood at the head of the Dale, a rambling nondescript building of grey stone with a greasy grey slate roof and mean little windows. It had been snowing in earnest for three nights, large curled flakes like goose down shrouding the world in one vast white blanket. Thick snow covered the fields, bent the black branches on the skeletal trees and gathered in great crusty billows behind the silvered limestone walls which criss-crossed the land. It was as if time had stood still, so silent and empty was the scene.

The farmer paced the flagstone floor inside, biting

his lower lip. Upstairs his wife, red-eyed with crying, sat with their young daughter, a delicate, red-faced child of eight who tossed and turned in the bed, her forehead wet with perspiration. The mother wiped the small face tenderly with a damp cloth and said a silent prayer over and over again.

The room downstairs had been decorated for Christmas. A large fir tree, draped in faded silver tinsel and a few wassailing balls, stood in a corner beneath which was a small pile of brightly-wrapped boxes. A crudely-made wooden crib containing small wooden figures of the Holy Family, the Magi and the shepherds had been placed on the mantle shelf and on the wall was an Advent calendar. The father stopped pacing the floor and stared at the crib. He thought of his young daughter, how she had unwrapped the Nativity figures and arranged them in the crib, how she had told him that this was going to be the best Christmas ever. His heart was heavy.

There were three heavy knocks on the farmhouse door. The woman upstairs heard the banging and left the child to join her husband at the foot of the stairs.

'John,' she whispered, her hand at her throat, 'who can it be on such a night?'

He didn't answer but stared at the door as if some dark and dangerous presence was without.

There were three more loud knocks.

'You must see who it is,' urged the wife. 'This is no night to be out.'

Her husband eased back the two bolts and turned the key. Cold air and a flurry of snow rushed through the door when it opened onto the dark night beyond. Standing framed in the doorway was a tall man in a shapeless black coat and a woollen hat which covered most of his face.

'Good God, man!' exclaimed the farmer. 'Whatever are you doing walking out on such a night as this?'

'I seek shelter,' said the man. His voice was soft, barely audible.

'Come in, come in,' said the woman moving forward and taking his arm. 'You'll catch your death of cold out there. John, close the door.'

The man entered the cottage. 'I thank you,' he said pulling of his woollen hat. 'It is good of you to give me shelter.'

'You are welcome,' said the woman.

The visitor was a striking-looking man with long lustrous shoulder length black hair and a dark beard. His eyes shone with intensity, bright brown eyes like those of a fox. 'I shall not stay long,' he said.

'You are welcome,' said the woman. 'You can't go out into the night again. You must stay until the snow clears.'

'Where were you heading on such a night?' asked the farmer. 'The snow is falling thick and fast, the roads are impassable and there is isn't another farmhouse for several miles.'

'I travel here and there,' said the stranger. 'I saw the light.'

'Come by the fire,' said the woman, 'and warm yourself. We have little to offer in the way of food but you are welcome to what we have. I'll make you a bowl of soup.'

'You are kind,' said the stranger.

'It's the least we can do,' replied the woman, smiling.

'How did you get here?' asked the farmer. 'The track is hidden beneath the snow.'

'I knew where the track would be.'

'The village is five miles away,' said the farmer. 'You can't have walked.'

'I walked,' said the stranger.

'But how did you find your way here on such a night as this?' he was asked.

'I saw the light,' repeated the stranger.

'No more questions John,' said the wife. 'Let the poor man get warm. I shall heat the soup. Then I must see to our daughter.'

'Your daughter,' repeated the stranger. He saw something dark and troubling in her eyes.

'She's very ill,' the farmer told him. 'We need the doctor but the tractor couldn't get through the snow. I tried.' His bottom lip began to tremble. 'I tried, I really tried but it got stuck. I couldn't find my way.'

'You will,' said the stranger. His manner was solicitous and kind.

'I'll get the soup,' said the woman.

The stranger stood by the fire staring into the flames. The farmer joined his wife in the kitchen.

'I don't know how he got here,' said the farmer. 'He can't have walked from the village. He would never have found the track and even if he had he would have frozen to death.'

'He's a strange man for sure,' said the wife. 'His eyes seem to look into your very soul. There's something about him. It's as if I know him and yet I have never seen him before. Don't you feel it, John?'

'I just cannot fathom it,' said the farmer, shaking his head. 'How could he have got here on such a night?'

They both turned. The stranger stood at the door.

'May I see your child?' he asked.

'She's so ill,' said the woman. There was a tremble in her voice and her eyes began to shine with tears. 'She has a fever.'

'I would like to see her,' said the stranger.

'Are you a doctor?' asked the farmer, hoping against hope that he was.

'I am not a doctor,' the stranger told him, 'but I would like to see your daughter.'

They took him to the child's bedroom. The girl twisted and turned in the bed and her face was still flushed and her forehead beaded with perspiration. Her breath came fast as if she were running a race.

The stranger knelt beside her and took her small hand in his and stroked it gently. The woman gave a small gasp for on the stranger's hands were dark red imprints as if they had been pierced. The child's breathing became more regular and she ceased to toss and turn. She then opened her eyes and smiled. 'Mama,' she said.

The stranger stood back.

'Thank God,' said the woman and held her child to her breast and rocked her gently.

The father stared at the stranger but uttered no words.

The farmer embraced his wife and child and the three clung to each other.

After a while the farmer stood and wiping his eyes with his fist turned to speak to the stranger. But their visitor had gone. Outside snowflakes pattered on the window panes and high in the sky a great shining star winked and a white moon lit up the world below.

'Who was he?' asked the farmer in a whisper.

'You know John,' said the woman tears trickling down her cheeks. 'You know.'

14

THE PARABLES

THE GOOD SAMARITAN

It was soon time for school assembly and I had agreed to talk to the children. I sat at the front of the hall with the Chairman of Governors, the local vicar on my right and the head teacher on my left. The children, crossed-legged and with expectant expressions on their faces, sat before me.

'One of the greatest storytellers that ever lived,' I began, 'changed people's lives with his wonderful stories. He never wrote them down, they were never put in a book during his lifetime and we have to depend upon his friends who heard him to know what he said. They weren't adventure stories or mysteries, horror stories or funny accounts, but everyone who heard them just had to listen. We know that this storyteller was a wonderful speaker, that hundreds of people would come to listen to him and to his fascinating tales, and we know that his stories told us how to treat others and how to live good lives. Does anyone know who I am talking about?'

'Jesus!' chorused the children.

'Yes, it's Jesus, and although Jesus never wrote down any of his stories, his friends did, and millions of people have read what he said nearly two thousand years ago. Jesus wanted everyone to be kind and love each other and was often surrounded by people who did not have much money, people who had done wrong, people who had got into trouble, people who were sick and lonely and people who were looked down upon by the rich and powerful.'

I held up a large red book. 'This children, is my bible, given to me by my parents when I was about your age. In it are all the stories of Jesus and they are called parables. Soon I shall read one of the stories called *The Parable of the Good Samaritan* from my red bible but first I am going to tell you the story. Now I want you all to listen very,

very carefully and when I read the story later on you will notice that certain things are not exactly the same as in the story I first told you. You see stories change in the telling and I guess that the disciple who wrote this story down changed things a little.'

I began. 'On a dusty road to Jericho on a hot, hot day a man fell among thieves. They beat him and stripped him and robbed him and left him for dead at the side of the road. That day along came three people. The first was a priest and when he saw the man, rather than going to help him, he crossed the road and walked by on the other side.'

All the children looked accusingly at the vicar.

'Next along the road came a teacher and he too crossed the road and went by on the other side.'

Now all eyes were on the head teacher.

'You see, children, sometimes the people who tell us how to behave don't do it themselves. They are called hypocrites.' Both the vicar and the head teacher shifted uncomfortably in their chairs. 'Now the third person to come along the road was a Samaritan, a member of a tribe of people not well-liked at the time of Jesus. The Samaritan did not cross the road but went to help the man and he took him to an inn where he paid for the innkeeper to look after him. "When I come this way again," he said, "if you have spent more money looking after the man, then I will pay you." Now Jesus asked those who had heard him speak which of these three they thought was the most caring. Which one do you think it was children?'

The children chorused, 'The Samaritan.'

'Yes it was the Good Samaritan. Now I am going to read the story as it was written down by one of the friends of Jesus.'

When I had finished I held high the red bible like some preacher of old, 'And what would you say to Jesus, if he were to walk into the hall this morning?' I asked.

A boy on the front row thought for a moment, then raised his hand and said loudly, 'I'd give 'im that book what you are 'oldin', Mester Phinn, and I'd say, "Jesus Christ – this is your life!"'

THE WIDOW'S MITE

It is not that Yorkshire people are parsimonious, as is sometimes claimed. They are thrifty and children are brought up, as I was, to be careful with their money as a head teacher new to the County was soon to find out.

At his first assembly the head teacher decided to tell the parable of *The Widow's Mite*.

'There was once a poor widow and when it came to put some money in the plate in church she put just a couple of copper coins, not worth very much at all. Also in the church was a very rich man and he put a lot more money in the plate. Now Jesus told his disciples that in the eyes of God the poor widow gave far more than the rich man for he gave only a very small part of his fortune but she gave everything she had in the world.'

A hand shot up. 'I reckon she didn't come from Yorkshire, sir,' observed a boy with a cheeky grin on his face.

As I listened to the retelling of this parable I was

reminded of an extract from the Reverend Francis Kilvert's diary, written in 1875:

Speaking to the children at the school about the Collect for the 2nd Sunday after the Epiphany and God's Peace, I asked them what beautiful image and picture of peace we have in the XXXIII psalm.

'The Good Shepherd,', said I, 'leading the sheep to . . . ?'
'to the slaughter,' said Frederick Herriman promptly.

One day I asked the children to what animal is our Saviour compared in the Bible. Frank Matthews confidently held out his hand.

'To an ass,' he said.

THE PRODIGAL SON

In the school assembly the head teacher, Mr Greenaway, a small man with large expressive hands and a deep resonant voice, related *The Parable of the Prodigal Son*.

'There was once a farmer who had two sons,' he boomed. 'One day, the younger son said to him: "Father, will you give me my share of your property?" The father agreed and divided all he owned and gave half to his son. The young man sold it and left home with a bulging purse and a light heart.' The head teacher continued with the story, telling the children how the younger son had squandered all his money and then had returned home penniless, ashamed and repentant, with his head held low. He told them how the father, with great happiness in his heart and with tears of joy in his eyes, had run to meet his son and how he had put his finest robe around his shoulders, sent his servant for his best sandals and ordered the fatted calf to be killed for a splendid feast to celebrate his son's homecoming. He paused momentarily, then continued, loudly and dramatically:

'And when the elder son heard the sound of the music and laughter and the news that his brother had returned, he was not pleased and would not enter the house. His father was saddened about this but his elder son told him angrily, "I have worked like a slave all these years for you, yet you have never even offered me so much as a goat for a feast with my friends. Now my good-for-nothing brother, who has spent all your money, turns up and you kill the fatted calf for him." The father had replied, "My son, you are with me all the time and everything I have is yours. Is it wrong that we should celebrate your brother's homecoming? My son was dead but now he is alive, he was lost but now he is found."'

Mr Greenaway spread wide his arms. 'Now children,' he said, 'who do you think was the happiest of all?' There was a forest of hands. He picked a small girl in the front row.

'The father!' she cried.

'That's right, Katy, and who do you think was the saddest and most disappointed about the son's return?'

Before he could pick anyone, a large boy at the back shouted out, 'Well, I reckon t'fatted calf can't 'ave been too 'appy.'

THE LOST SHEEP

At Holmdale Junior and Infant School, situated deep in a secluded place in the heart of the North York Moors and surrounded on all sides by rugged moorland, the local Baptist minister, an evangelical young man wearing a T-shirt with 'Fight truth decay – study the Bible every day' on the front, re-told *The Parable of The Lost Sheep*. He started well, immediately capturing the children's interest. The great majority of his audience came from farming families so at the mention of sheep all ears pricked up.

'When Jesus was alive,' he told them, 'sheep were very important in the lives of people.'

'They still are,' said one rosy-cheeked girl, sitting near at the front.

'Yes, indeed,' continued the minister. 'And in those days, sheep provided meat and milk and cheese. But pasture was poor on the hills—'

'Not too good up here, either,' said the girl.

'No,' agreed the minister. 'So pasture was poor on the

hills and the shepherd had to move his flock from place to place to find grass for his sheep. Unlike today, the shepherd at the time when Jesus lived did not drive his flock in front of him but led it and he knew each of his sheep personally and they answered to his call.'

There were several sceptical looks and furrowed brows at this point. 'How many would he have in his flock, then?' asked a boy of about ten or eleven with a shock of red hair.

'Well, in the parable I'm going to tell you in a minute, the shepherd has a hundred sheep,' replied the minister.

'He's not likely to know an 'undred sheep personally,' observed the boy. 'Cows, mebbe, but not sheep.'

'Well, I . . . the shepherd . . . he probably would have known his sheep very well.'

'But not an 'undred!'

'Let's make a start on the story and then we can talk about it afterwards, shall we?' said the minister, looking a little uneasy. I could see from his expression that he was unused to members of his congregation shouting out and commenting at every turn. This was clearly not his usual captive audience. 'Now, if any of those sheep strayed, the shepherd would search for them until he found them.'

'He wanted a good collie-dog,' said the red-haired boy. 'Save a lot o' time and trouble.'

'Aye,' nodded a few of his companions.

The minister carried on regardless and speeded up his delivery, hoping by doing so to discourage any further interruptions. 'The shepherd protected his sheep from wild animals and thieves by using a catapult and a wooden club—'

'Shotgun would 'ave been better,' remarked a child.

'And at night,' continued the minister, ignoring the observation, 'the shepherd kept his flock in a stone-walled sheepfold topped with thorns and he would block the entrance by lying across it.'

'I can't see my dad doing that,' said the girl at the front, laughing.

'Now this parable is called *The Lost Sheep* and it was told by Jesus nearly two thousand years ago.' The minister took a deep breath, rubbed his hands, smiled and began. 'There was once a shepherd and he had a hundred sheep. One day he discovered that one of the sheep had strayed.

He could have said, "Ah well, I have ninety-nine so why should I bother searching high and low, hither and thither, for just one sheep. If I leave the other sheep they will be at the mercy of wolves and thieves. Anyway, the lost sheep might be dead by now." But the shepherd did not say this, for every single one of his sheep was precious to him. So he went in search of the one lost sheep.'

'Hardly worth the effort, price of lamb being what it is at t'moment,' commented the rosy-faced girl.

'This was quite a long time ago,' the minister informed her, still managing to retain his smile. 'So, the shepherd left the ninety-nine and went in search of the one lost sheep.'

'What breed o' sheep were they, then?' asked the girl.

'Breed?' repeated the minister.

'Aye, what breed?'

'Well, does it make a difference?' he asked.

'It makes an 'ell of a lot o' difference. Some sheep are docile, others are reight frisky. If you're talking 'Erdwicks, they never shift, they'll stop where they are till t'cows come home. We've got 'Erdwicks. They're a Cumbrian breed. They may be small but they're tough and eat owt that's going – grass, nettles, couch grass – owt. Now, if t'shepherd left a flock of 'Erdwicks e'd still find 'em theer when 'e got back.'

'I see,' said the minister lamely and wrinkling his forehead into a frown.

'In t'gret freeze o' 1947,' continued the girl blithely, ''Erdwicks were t'only breed what survived up 'ere.'

'How old are you?' asked the minister.

'Eight,' replied the child. 'Anyroad, in t'gret freeze o' 1947 'Erdwicks ate bits of 'eather what stuck up above snow an' managed to live 'til t'shepherd got to'em but all t'other breeds ended up deead.'

'Well, I shouldn't imagine that the sheep were Herdwicks,' interrupted the minister keen to get in with the parable.

'But what I'm sayin',' persisted the girl, 'is that if t'shepherd left a flock of 'Erdwicks he'd still find 'em theer when 'e got back.'

'Yes I see,' started the minister, 'but –'

'But if you're talking Leicesters,' continued the girl, 'they'd be leaping all ovver t'show. They'd be off as soon as shepherd's turned 'is back.'

'That's why tha needs a good collie-dog,' insisted the boy with the red hair.

'So what breed were they?' asked the girl.

'Well,' said the minister, having a sudden flash of inspiration, 'these were Palestine Blues, a very lively breed.'

'Never 'eard of them,' commented the girl sulkily. 'What do they look like?'

'Oh big and woolly and white,' began the minister feebly. He pressed on quickly to prevent any further interruptions and awkward questions. 'What joy the shepherd felt when he found his lost sheep. He put it on his shoulders and hurried back to tell everyone his good news and invite his friends to share his happiness.'

'And were his other sheep still there?' asked the boy with the red hair.

'Indeed, they were, and the shepherd was very happy.

Without pausing, the minister clasped his hands together and said very quickly, 'Now why do you think he went in search of just one sheep?' I guess he hoped that the children would appreciate the meaning of the parable, that every single one of us is valuable in the eyes of God and that 'there is more joy in heaven when one sinner turns back to God than ninety-nine who see no need to repent'. But the point was missed.

'Why do you think the shepherd risked losing all the other sheep just for the one which was lost?' he asked again.

The vociferous little girl raised a hand. ''Appen it were t'tup!' she said.

15

THE TEACHER

THE SMALL PIECE OF PAPER

It was on one cold, raw day, a week before the schools broke up for the Christmas holidays that I was scheduled to visit a small village primary school deep in the Dales. That morning the sky was an empty, steely grey and the air so icy it almost burnt your cheeks and ears. The drive from the nearby market town up a narrow, twisting, slippery road was memorable. Ahead of me were long belts of dark green firs with a light dusting of powdery snow, glistening in an ocean of dark heather, silvered limestone walls, with misty peaks rising majestically in the distance. It was a tranquil and beautiful world.

I guess it was because I was so taken with the scene before me and not concentrating on where I was going that I took a wrong turn. It was then that I came upon the chapel: a small, squat building of dark grey stone with mean little windows and a sagging roof. Next to it was an overgrown graveyard full of tilting tombstones and neglected graves. To my surprise the chapel was open and having a little time to spare before my appointment at the school I decided to spend a few minutes looking around. The interior, dim and damp and icy cold, was spartan – a worn unpolished wooden floor, heavy, dark wooden pews and plain white walls. This chapel, I thought, was probably built some three hundred and fifty years' ago for a group of dissenters. I imagined those stern-faced joyless Puritans soberly observant who refused to celebrate Christmas and condemned those who did. I could see them in their plain black clothes praying earnestly in the uncomfortable pews all those years ago.

As I made to leave I came upon a small piece of paper pinned to the door. The account was, like the parables of Jesus, a simply-expressed, powerful piece of writing containing the truth for many millions of people: that

Jesus Christ, born in poverty in a stable, is the greatest example of love that the world has ever seen:

He was born in an obscure village. He worked in a carpenter's shop until he was thirty. He then became an itinerant preacher. He never taught a lesson in a classroom. He had no tools to work with such as blackboards, maps or charts. He used no subject guidelines, kept no records, gave no grades and his only text was ancient and well-worn. His students were the poor, the lame, the outcasts, the deaf, and the blind. The content of his method was the same for all who came to hear him and to learn from him. He opened eyes with his faith, he opened hearts with love, a love born of forgiveness. A gentle man, a humble man, he asked for and he won no honours, no gold awards of merit to his expertise and wisdom. He never held an office. He never had a family or owned a house. He didn't go to college. He had no credentials but himself. He was only thirty-three when the public turned against him. His friends ran away. He was turned over to his enemies and went through the mockery of a trial. He was nailed to a

cross between two thieves. While he was dying his executioners gambled over his clothing, the only property he had on earth. He was laid in a borrowed grave. All the armies that have ever marched, all the navies that have ever sailed, all the parliaments that have ever sat and all the monarchs that have ever reigned have not affected the life of man as much as he. For this quiet teacher from the hills of Galilee has fed the needs, fulfilled the hopes and changed the lives of many millions. For what he taught brought heaven to earth and revealed God's heart to mankind.

16

A CHRISTMAS BLESSING

God bless the father of this house
And God bless the mother,
God bless the sister of this house
And God bless the brother.
God bless family and friends
Who live both far and near
And a happy Christmas to you all
And a prosperous New Year.

The poems, 'The Visit of the School Inspector', 'No Room at the Inn', 'A Special Time of the Year', 'The Colour of Christmas' and 'A Visit to the Pantomime' first appeared in *Alien in the Classroom* published by Andersen Press (2010). 'The Little Angel' first appeared in *The Day our Teacher went Batty* (2002) and 'Treasure' first appeared in *It Takes One to Know One* (2001), both collections published by Puffin Books. 'A Christmas Miracle' is based on an Irish folk tale, 'The Christmas Visitor'.

Discover Gervase Phinn's heart-warming *Little Village School* series

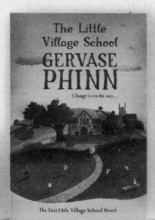

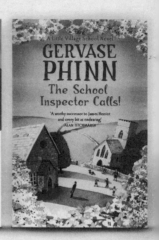

'Packed with delightful and authentic characters, juicy gossip, precarious romance and good old-fashioned village drama'
Good Book Guide

'A worthy successor to James Herriot and every bit as endearing'
Alan Titchmarsh

f Gervase Phinn

Visit the official Facebook fan page for all the latest book news